wayne
B E N N E T T

LEAGUE'S A LOT LIKE LIFE

WITH STEVE CRAWLEY

PACIFIC SPORTS

P R O D U C T I O N S

HarperSports

An imprint of HarperCollins*Publishers*

Harper*Sports*
An imprint of HarperCollins*Publishers*

First published in Australia in 1996
by HarperCollins*Publishers* Pty Limited
ACN 009 913 517
A member of the HarperCollins*Publishers* (Australia) Pty Limited Group

HarperCollins*Publishers*
25 Ryde Road, Pymble, Sydney, NSW 2073, Australia
31 View Road, Glenfield, Auckland 10, New Zealand
77–85 Fulham Palace Road, London W6 8JB, United Kingdom
Hazelton Lanes, 55 Avenue Road, Suite 2900, Toronto, Ontario M5R 3L2
and 1995 Markham Road, Scarborough, Ontario M1B 5M8, Canada
10 East 53rd Street, New York NY 10032, USA

National Library of Australia Cataloguing-in-Publication data:

Bennett, Wayne, 1950 —.

  League's a lot like life.

  ISBN 0 7322 5725 5.

  1. Bennett, Wayne, 1950 — Philosophy. 2. Rugby
  League football — Australia. I. Title.

796.338

All articles reproduced courtesy of *The Weekend Australian*.

All photos courtesy of *Rugby League Week*
except for Wally Lewis photo, courtesy of Clifford White.

Printed in Australia by Griffin Paperbacks, Adelaide.

9 8 7 6 5 4 3 2 1
00 99 98 97 96

CONTENTS

THE AUTHORS

Wayne Bennett was born on the rich Downs country of Queensland.

In senior rugby league, he represented Queensland and later coached his beloved state to Origin glory.

Canberra plucked him from the Brisbane coaching scene in 1987 and with coach Don Furner the Raiders made the grand final the very same year. In 1988 Bennett returned to Brisbane and a new establishment called the Broncos.

Bennett and the Broncos scored successive Winfield Cup premierships in 1992–93, and together they are still at it.

He is married to Trish and they have three children, Elizabeth, Katherine and Justin.

Economical with words and smiles, with Wayne Bennett, everything in life and league counts just the same.

Steve Crawley is recognised as being one of Australia's leading sports writers, having won several major awards for his writing on rugby league, horse racing and tennis.

He has held senior columnist positions with *The Sun*, *The Sydney Morning Herald*, *The Melbourne Herald Sun* and *The Australian*, and served as turf editor of *The Telegraph Mirror*, and sports editor of *The Sun Herald*.

In recent years, Steve has concentrated on television, heading up the sports department at Channel 10, where he developed and worked as the executive producer on Sports Tonight.

Steve is currently director of Pacific Sports Productions and sports editor for network Seven.

INTRODUCTION

BY STEVE CRAWLEY

Often people ask: "Who really writes Wayne Bennett's column?"

See, I'm the "with" bit at the end of every article. Together, we have been compiling these columns in *The Weekend Australian* since the Broncos' grand final triumph of 1993, their second in succession.

And, it's true, in the very beginning Wayne Bennett didn't *really* write it. Not all of it, anyway. But every week, as is his way, he contributed a little more . . . and more again.

Wayne Bennett is one of those guys people call self-educated. He left school at age 14 with no real education and not much else. In rugby league, as in life, he played the games straight and hard. Yet there is a softness, a simple understanding, cradled between the lines of his columns which provides a far greater insight to the man and to the coach than any old arithmetic test or reporter's microphone.

Here is a walking contradiction: he hates to talk about himself yet is so darn self-assured; his post-match press conferences border on being monosyllabic yet, privately, he reels off great quote after great quote; and he intimidates, props up, strengthens and softens those around him at the same time.

Outside of his circle — and his circle is small — Wayne Bennett remains pretty much misunderstood. Sing no sad songs for him, though, because that's his problem, the sneaking suspicion being that it's the way he likes it and planned it.

One of the great kicks he gets from his columns is the fact their appeal seemingly reaches far beyond the fields of rugby league and even football. Sure, South Sydney manager and top-rating broadcaster Alan Jones is said to collect them for his young Rabbitohs, and it's also apparently true that coach Kevin Sheedy has one framed on a wall of the Essendon dressing room, but it's the reactions of people you and I never hear about that make Wayne Bennett tap dance in the dark.

He makes no excuses for this book, *LEAGUE'S A LOT LIKE LIFE*. And it is *his* book. I just sit there. "With" him.

wayne
BENNETT

ON THE GAME OF LIFE

Our greatest challenge is to
be better than we were.

MAESTRO, LET THE MUSIC PLAY

APRIL 2, 1994

Entertaining the masses is something I never tried to do, though privately I'm a great one for cliches, with favourite sayings and words.

Instead of dropping them in the media, I prefer to keep them to myself, to my own thinking, at times sharing them with my players.

To me, it's better to speak for five or ten seconds than dribbling on for five minutes without getting the message across.

Some go back to my times in the police force, like:

Isn't it amazing how much can be accomplished when no-one cares who gets the credit?

A lot of people worry not about getting the job done but about who's going to get the credit. I've always said to the players: "Let's get the job done . . . and we'll all get some credit."

The media, like the fans, has its favourites. Some guys can just run on and be assured of a wrap. Others, they might not be fancy, but they're players you know are valuable to the team and its spirit. They must know that you know their value.

To be a champion, strive not to surpass your competitor but your previous self.

So many of us spend a lifetime wanting to have what someone else has, trying to beat somebody else.

Our greatest challenge is to be better than we were.

Let's say the Broncos win a premiership, it's not beating all those other teams — it's being better than we were.

Say an athlete's best time for the 100 is 10.3 and he runs a 10.25, a time he's strived to clock. He might finish the race third but, you see, he doesn't have to be first past the line to succeed. If you've got to win, you're left with nothing. There can only ever be one winner.

Most men die with the music inside them. Man, don't you die with the music inside you.

That's a life of potential never reached. The fellow who never practised as hard as he should

> **There are no great men – only great challenges which ordinary men are forced by circumstances to meet.**

have, who never made the sacrifices, who might have been . . .

It means don't go through life, whether it be relationships, sport — life — sitting down at the end and saying it could have been better. No-one is going to finish with a clean slate, having realised every bit of potential. Still, there's no reason why some slates should be so bloody dirty.

There are no great men – only great challenges which ordinary men are forced by circumstances to meet.

Often we hear the comment: "Isn't he a great man?"

Perhaps he is, perhaps he's done some great things. The assumption is he was born great.

I read a wonderful article in the last *Weekend Australian* about Weary Dunlop, how when the challenge came he met it. Now they say what a great man he was. Weary Dunlop was, in fact, an ordinary man but he met the great challenges where other people might well have walked away from them.

The most successful people I've met are the ones who handle adversity in the right manner.

For most people, two or three times a year in relationships or business they're going to face some high drama. Handled wrongly, the damage can be irreparable.

The ones who handle it right solve it so much more quickly. They're the ones who get on with their lives.

The highest reward for a person's toil is not what they get for it but what they become by it.

So often the question is: "How much am I going to get paid?" When it should be: "What will I become by it?"

Accept criticism and disappointment as a part of life and when it comes stand up straight, look it in the eyes and say you cannot defeat me — I am bigger than you.

Self-explanatory, as is my other favourite, a piece by Dale Winbrow, titled: "The Man in the Glass".

When you get what you want in this struggle for self,
And the world makes you king for a day,
Then go to your mirror and look at yourself,
And see what that man has to say.
For it isn't your father, your mother, or wife,
Whose judgment of you — you must pass,
The fellow whose verdict counts most in your life,
Is the guy staring back in the glass.
He is the man you must please — never mind all the rest,
For he's with you clear up to the end.
And you have passed your most difficult and dangerous test,
When the man in the glass is your friend,
You can be like another and chisel a plum,
And think you're a wonderful guy,
But the man in the glass says you're only a bum,
If you can't look him straight in the eye.
You can fool the whole world, down the pathway of years,
And get pats on your back as you pass,
But your final reward will be heartaches and tears,
If you've cheated the man in the glass.

GET ON THE BUS, KID, IF YOU WANT TO PLAY THE GAME OF LIFE

JULY 8, 1995

Fulltime professionalism in sport sounds, well, professional.

It's an issue I studied three or four years ago, long before the salary boom in rugby league: an issue on which I've very strong opinions.

Footballers differ from Olympians in that our game is contested every weekend for up to eight months of the year, whereas Olympians set themselves for only three or four events a year.

Olympians train rigorously twice a day and genuinely need plenty of rest in between.

If they're not training, they're sleeping or eating. They have neither the time nor the energy to hold down a real job.

Several times I've been to America looking at gridiron and its fulltime professionalism.

Been to the UK looking at soccer, too.

Because of their strong work ethic, in America they make the players fill up the whole day studying: things like videos of themselves and their rivals. "Xs and Os", as they call them.

From eight in the morning to four in the afternoon, six days a week, they train physically only once a day.

Don't worry, there's lots to fill their days.

I've been in those classrooms and the players who aren't asleep owe it to copious amounts of black coffee.

The coach? He just keeps talking.

Like with most staff meetings, they eventually walk out with all the problems still existing but the boss always feeling better.

In the UK I saw some contrast. At one club the players come in at 10 o'clock, have no lectures, train, and are home at one. Every day.

At the other club I visited they come in at nine, go through the classroom stuff, the videos, lunch together and train in the afternoon. At three, they bundy off.

Sure I asked the coaches: Why? One said he worries like anything what his players might be doing afterwards.

After knocking off, he roams the clubs and bars, driving time and again past the all-night parties praying not to see a familiar face.

Another coach worries about his players' insular lifestyles, that they don't mix with anybody bar footballers.

No-one works their hours and because they don't mix they could get very bitchy, inward: the little things invariably becoming mountainous issues.

It's not unlike people who never leave a small town. Born there, die there. They think they know everyone's business, yet on the world scale of things they know little.

Anyway, I came away from those situations determined fulltime professionalism was not for me or my players.

I find little value in being able to play sport but not life.

In the US National Football League there's merit in the college system because the players have some kind of degree and life skills behind them by the time they turn pro at 22 or 23.

> **I find little value in being able to play sport but not life.**

Those apprentices in English soccer, that's sad. Some as young as 16, hoping to make it against all hope. They get bundled out of the system at 19.

I'm sure they can still kick a ball but suddenly there are no goalposts, and their only chance of a career is a car out of control.

Look at the kid who quits school at 14 and nine months. He's 45kg. He's going to be the next Mick Dittman. By 18, he's 75kg.

His old mates are at Uni, his new ones are riding in races against Dittman. He's sitting in the stands, the public stands, with no job and not much else.

We have a greater responsibility to our young players than to promise them all glitter, and deliver no more than a grunt and a door with "no entry" on the other side.

Sportspeople don't live in the real world. They have managers running around for them, people rubbing them down, spit-polishing their boots, doing their banking, generally sorting out their problems. So comes the day their playing careers are over. They're 30. It's not easy to grow up at 30, and even as fulltimers I doubt we could train one more minute than we do now, not when we play every Sunday.

> **We have a policy at our club concerning younger players. No work, no play.**

To me, the ideal situation is for the established players to work three or four hours a day, just enough to get them out of bed.

Younger players we encourage to get careers, to work their eight hours a day before training. Whether they be at college or doing apprenticeships, you'll see them turning up come May or June looking very tired.

We have a policy at our club concerning younger players. No work, no play.

A lot of these kids turning up tired, they're not going to make it in football but, as I tell their parents, we don't want them to be failures in life.

Players have to get away from football so when it comes time to play they're looking forward to the game, the contest.

We want them stimulated, not sour. We want them out on the street facing up to their public when they've played both well and badly.

It's never a bad thing for them to face the music rather than hiding behind the classroom doors with their robot team-mates.

There can be no guarantees in our game, and while I see the younger players questioning the outside work requirements I still rest knowing some of the most talented kids I've seen never made it.

I have a friend whose 15-year-old son only ever used to come out of the surf to go to school, eat and sleep, and at times he didn't even come out for that school part.

> **"Just get on the bus, kid, and enjoy the ride as much as you can."**

He got offered a job a couple of afternoons and Saturday mornings at $4.50 an hour.

By the time he'd paid his bus fare from school to work and home again there was only small change, and the boy questioned the job's value.

His dad said: "One day you'll understand — just get on the bus."

The old man's right: "Just get on the bus, kid, and enjoy the ride as much as you can."

Landing in it can prove downright insightful

June 3, 1995

A million miles from Brookvale Oval, I was chasing cows this morning on my mate's farm, wondering what would happen if I ever caught one of them.

The big thing about tough matches like tomorrow's against the unbeaten Manly-Warringah is to be ready on the day, not a day or days before. Often teams make their speeches long before the dinner, and have nothing left to say.

When we went to Brookvale for this corresponding match last year, they were playing very well, the Broncos not so well, and they deserved their win.

All the same, we got a very tough time from the referee and the only thing I ask this time round is for a fair deal. It would be nice for the referee not to influence the result.

You think the strangest things, chasing cows. Like the note my daughter came home from school with just the other day. She'd been listening to Vicki Wilson, the Australian netballer. Vicki had said: "If you always do what you've always done you'll always get what you've always got."

I liked that one so much I took it to the players, reminding a few I've been a little tough on lately that they have to change because if they don't they will never get better, never reach the heights I believe they can.

There's always room for improvement — it's the biggest room in the house. Cliches. Win without boasting, lose without excuse.

9

Don't brag, for it's not the whistle that moves the train.

That's a good one when you're winning.

There's another: The bigger a man's head gets, the easier it is to fill his shoes. Ain't that the truth. But not everyone wins.

The other day I wrote this to a friend in jail, a footballing friend. He'd asked me for some thoughts to help him through a pretty tough time, and I didn't need much paper.

"A 'no' uttered from the deepest conviction is better than a 'yes' merely uttered to please, or, what is worse, to avoid trouble." And then I put in brackets: "If you had said no mate, you wouldn't be where you are today."

I rarely take much notice of critics or criticism, not unless it's justified, for the majority of critics know not victory or defeat.

To borrow from Theodore Roosevelt: "Better it is to dare mighty things, to win glorious triumphs even though checkered with failure, than to rank with those poor spirits who neither enjoy much or suffer much, because they live in the great twilight that knows not victory or defeat." Go Theodore.

Go Nelson Mandela, too. He spoke on one of my favourites, forgiveness.

"The weak can never forgive," he said. "Forgiveness is the attitude of the strong."

Mr Mandela also got it right about the fact that we can never forget, but must forgive, especially sitting opposite your adversary.

> **"The weak can never forgive. Forgiveness is the attitude of the strong."**
> NELSON MANDELA

Some 99 per cent of failure comes from people who practise the habit of making excuses. So many coaches around the world have echoed the words of the NFL's Chuck Noll: "We tell our players that if they are going to point a finger, to point it at the mirror. The attitude has to be, 'If we're not winning, it is my fault'."

I, too, have been to too many staff meetings where it was someone else's fault. And I've had more trouble with myself than with any other man I've met.

In my life, I notice a lot of people advising others how to run their lives but still haven't got their own act together. Our greatest challenge is ourselves. Until we master ourselves, any words in the direction of helping others are worth no more than what I just put my foot in, chasing cows.

DEFENSIVE EDGE FAVOURS SEA EAGLES IN FINALE

SEPTEMBER 23, 1995

Sunday too far away. Such a special day for the players, for everybody involved.

It's what all 20 clubs strive for, but 18 miss out.

I hate football at the moment, the Broncos not being part of it. I love AFL now.

But for Manly and Bulldog fans, good luck to them.

The unseen if not unsung heroes of this are the families of the players and officials. They make a lot of sacrifices throughout the season and know how important it is right now for their husbands and sons.

It's a great occasion. When you've done a lot of things in football, played first grade and represented a bit, above it all it's these grand finals that kind of make it seem and feel worthwhile. It's an emotional time.

I know in my mum's case, when we played in those grand finals she refused to listen to the radio or watch TV. No-one was allowed to ring her.

Mum would wait till five o'clock and put the radio on, but only briefly. It was the only way she could handle it. It can be very traumatic.

What do I miss most? The event. That special feeling in the week leading up. It's what you've trained for. It's just about everything.

Really irking me this week is the great emphasis on this being an "all-Sydney" decider. So what? This is not about Sydney versus

Brisbane or Newcastle or Canberra, or whatever . . . this is a national competition and should be viewed that way.

For the Broncos, it was when we got on the plane but being Sydney-based for Manly and the Bulldogs the relief will come when they finally get on the bus bound for the ground.

From Saturday morning on, after that last training session, the hardest part is the wait.

You just wish to play it at nine o'clock in the morning.

So when you get on the bus it's not far away, and the rest just clicks into place. It's virtually routine now.

Anybody who says playing in a grand final and winning isn't one of the best feelings of all hasn't won one.

It's the ultimate. It deserves every accolade, and I don't think there is a word or feeling that can overdo it.

The one thing that struck me in grand finals, or after them anyway, there's this reflection on the enormous amount of sacrifice and work which has gone into that one performance and you know the game's not really won on that Sunday afternoon.

> **Anybody who says playing in a grand final and winning isn't one of the best feelings of all hasn't won one.**

Go back to November, to December, the previous January or February, to that torturous hill some trainer found or the outback ground with no fans and no cheers, just self-sacrifice and a determination to get the job done.

Go back to the sheer exhaustion, to asking yourself, is it worth going through all of this for that one final moment? And then, two weeks later, it's over and you're having to look at the next one.

That's why some teams and some guys never go back and play in grand finals, because they don't get it out of their system. They're still living on and for that one afternoon in September.

And, of course, there is a great danger for the losing guys as well, because they sit there asking themselves: Why have I nothing tangible to show for it?

So they spend the entire off-season asking themselves: Was it all worth it?

When you win, no, I'm never happy for myself. Feelings vary with different coaches and different philosophies but the first time we won I just felt very lucky, very humbled to have come from Queensland country with no special qualifications and be part of a Winfield Cup grand final I'd only dreamt about a decade before . . . to be part of it with such a wonderful group of men.

In life, if you're going to do or say something, first of all make sure you're a winner.

The best part, or feeling, is the family. They believed all along and suddenly don't have to put up with the smart alecs and knockers, not for three or four months at least.

You're never going to shut them up forever but there is no comeback with a grand final triumph and that is a glorious feeling, particularly for family and friends.

All of a sudden you don't have to go around justifying your players and your club to anyone.

In life, if you're going to do or say something, first of all make sure you're a winner.

After the game, the win, you go around that stadium and come home through airports and realise what it means to people, you feel happy for them.

A lot of people live their winters, their lives, through football, you see it in their faces, and that is what makes it such a passionate game.

I first saw it in State of Origin, and sensed it at Souths in Brisbane where everything seemed so small compared to what happens in the Winfield Cup.

By Monday morning, one lot of fans will be waking up in heaven while the other mob cope with their emptiness.

I can't go past Manly. Canterbury have done everything right, they're playing tough, but Manly's defence has been bloody impressive. And they've done it all season.

On the other hand, the Bulldogs allowed in only one try against Canberra, two against the Broncos and one against St George. It's a pretty mean effort.

Canterbury's fine asset is that they are playing well and for each other, and they're going to be tough to beat.

I liked Chris Anderson, their coach, when he was a player and I like him now. He's a practical guy and he makes his players tough.

I just noticed some of the things said by the Canterbury players this week, how they've learned to publicly treat it as just another game of football.

You know it's not, but everything has to be in perspective. If you put any more emphasis on it it'll just blow you away.

It's double-dutch, or coach-talk, saying something when you know something else to be true, and it's ridiculous to think it's just another game because it's not.

But to make it into a bigger event, when it's already so huge, that's a psychological blowout.

By taking the other approach, the momentum of the week will hype the players but it will be controlled hype.

Once on the field, more than anywhere else, it is just another game with play-the-balls, running and passing.

Players might look back and realise they'd played in tougher games, and I think Mal Meninga said exactly that after last year's grand final, but they've got to be ready to accept that. If it comes easy, take it. Which ever way it comes, just be ready for it.

I think this will be a defence-oriented grand final, but that doesn't mean there won't be a blowout of 20 or 30 points at the end of the day.

A couple of quick tries, and it could all be over.

It will be a very emotional day. There's not a lot of love between these two clubs. No clubs love each other, but I think it's a bit more personal with Manly and Canterbury.

Not a lot has been said, but I think it's simmering.

If it comes easy, take it. Which ever way it comes, just be ready for it.

I like Manly's defence, and they have a great competitor in Geoff Toovey. He'll just aim them up all day.

For Canterbury, the word to remember is patience. Against

sides with great defence it's so easy to become frustrated and begin pushing plays, so Canterbury just can't afford to get disappointed if they come up empty early.

They just have to keep coming back, going back and building, coming back at them again.

I'll watch it — but I'm not going. I wouldn't put myself through that.

ROLES CHANGE BUT CHARACTER REMAINS CONSISTENT

AUGUST 19, 1995

Often we talk about how much rugby league has changed, particularly in the past 20 years. The role of many positions on the field has changed as dramatically as anything, but the great characters still epitomise their respective positions.

No better place to start than the front-row.

Without front-rowers and their ability to do a job you can't have a football team of any quality.

The first thing every club boss in every country town will ask when you walk in is: "You wouldn't know where we could find a front-rower?"

I believe this position is the toughest to play. Twenty years ago, they were simply the enforcers of the game and, I guess, to a lesser extent that is still part of their job. But stiff arms, boxing matches and softening-up periods have been replaced by sustained, aggressive defence and power hitting — all within the rules.

Front-rowers have to be very single-minded. Often they don't possess great speed and in most cases, no great evasive skills either. So whether the team wins by 50 points or loses by two, there is still no easy way out for the front-rower.

I think the great ones had a lot of character about them. Take Arthur Beetson; he had tremendous mobility and tremendous skills. Great hands. He was one of the greatest because Arthur had that little bit more.

When I say front-rowers are different, you only need to have followed the careers of people like Martin Bella, big Blocker (Roach), Sammy (Backo) . . . but I suppose one of the endearing characteristics about the majority of front-rowers is that they always engage their mouths before their brains.

They're classics. Once on tour in New Zealand someone made a reference to all the sheep there and Blocker said: "Yeah, you can get as much pork as you want here."

Sammy Backo. Ah, Sammy. We were coming home one night and the pilot informs us we will be 15 or 20 minutes late into Brisbane because of a very strong headwind. As we were coming into Brisbane, the pilot returns to say that he's been able to increase speed and we'll indeed be arriving on time.

Sammy turns and says, "Coach, it's a good thing that headwind was with us."

Sam Backo is still trying to work out how come everyone dies in alphabetical order.

Second-rowers. I can't say a lot about second-rowers. They're like 1000 lifesavers. They are very dependable guys.

One position which has really changed is hooker. When I played, the hooker's job was to get dummy-half, to pass and tackle.

The modern hooker is more like a halfback of 20 years ago. They would all be fine halfbacks but not great halfbacks, lacking just a little flair. Still, they're cheeky like the No. 7s, usually tough too.

> **I can't say a lot about second-rowers. They're like 1000 lifesavers. They are very dependable guys.**

Locks. Now here's a role that has changed. When you talk of great lock-forwards, the names John Raper and Ron Coote spring to mind. But it's different today because the lock no longer has to cover defend. They're usually tall, rangy, with great pace and clever with the ball. We have just described Bradley Clyde.

Traditionally in this game, if your lock is OK and your halfback is OK and your five-eighth is OK the team is better than OK.

Halfback. I have never coached nor seen a good halfback who wasn't cheeky, and I sometimes worry about that characteristic. The halfback is the catalyst of all things, on and off the field.

If I go to recruit a halfback and he's not cheeky — there's not a bit of rogue about him — I tend to drift away. Again I think his size makes him what he is. He's been a bit of a dwarf since childhood, the butt of a lot of fun and jokes, so his personality has developed around that.

> **If I go to recruit a halfback and he's not cheeky — there's not a bit of rogue about him — I tend to drift away.**

Five-eighths are usually good steady types of people, often the steadying influence on a club. The great ones, because of the sacrifices they have to make for the team, are great team men.

Centres. Tremendous speed and flair, and can be prima donnas. If Chris Johns had any prima donna in him, Kevin Walters knocked it out early by throwing him terrible passes and having him knocked out. I believe the hardest place on the field to defend.

Wingers. This position has changed more than most. Once they were purely finishers, waiting for the ball: now, with all the kicking, they are much more involved.

I think the fullback has to be mentally tough. He's in the situation where everyone sees every mistake he makes. A lot of the time he has little or no control and if he dwells on his mistake, he's gone for the rest of the game.

With the game as it is today I reckon the backs could play twice a week but after one match you'd be looking for another pack of forwards.

Whenever I have moved a back into the forwards he has walked off at fulltime with two comments: "I'll never drop the ball again; and please don't put me back there again."

I have noticed many more athletes coming into our game, but coming into it without football sense.

Footballers know where to put the ball, they know where there's a gap, how to read a game — but the athlete knows none of this. The things I talk about, the know-how, it has been learned in the backyard.

If we're not very careful and we trade the football instinct for athleticism, the game is going to get pretty boring.

The other guy can run all day and looks great with his shirt off but he plays pretty dumb.

As my mate says, you can't put brains in monuments.

Watching Life Unfold Can Be Trying

July 15, 1995

Spectator? Look, I go to the football every weekend but the last time I went as a spectator, with popcorn in my mouth and fun in the heart, was back in November '94, the day that the Denver Broncos played the Kansas City Chiefs.

Rightly or wrongly, I have a pretty dour image when it comes to sitting in the stands at rugby league matches, and, it's true, I do see it as my office.

Everything I have done all week rides on Sunday, the only day of the week I have so little control over, yet with everything depending on it.

The difficult thing about coaching is that the players can — and you can — do a great job all week only to see it fall to bits on Sunday.

I remember Jack Gibson saying Sunday was his day off, but could never quite work out that one.

I've been there, to the wall, a lot of times but still on many days I'm nervous, shadow-boxing butterflies.

Once I used to watch like a fan. No more. As they say: "If you begin listening to the fans it won't be long before you're sitting with them."

Often, I can't see what the opposition's doing and after a game when someone says so-and-so had a great match for them, I just hunch my shoulders, say, "right".

To me, the enjoyment is after the game. Those five minutes,

21

that half an hour. Maybe even the whole night. That is something you cannot replace being a spectator.

There are two questions I get most asked, the first one being: Are you going to win today? As if I know. It fascinates me how punters go up to horse trainers, asking: "How's Radish going to aim up today?" All the trainer knows is that Radish has trained well, he hasn't a clue how Licorice from the other stable is feeling.

The second most asked question is: What did you say to them at halftime? To be honest, I have two speeches, the same as all the coaches — one when we're winning: one when we're losing.

But if I could sneak out of the house, in beanie and scarf, not caring what I said or thought all afternoon, there are at least five sportspeople in the world I would seek out for entertainment and inspiration alone.

> **"I can accept failure, everyone fails at something. But I can't accept not trying."**
> MICHAEL JORDAN

The first is Boris Becker, he of the crappy haircut and majestic longevity. The consistency. Boris Becker was winning Wimbledon a decade ago, as a teenager buying mansions in Monte Carlo. Yet he's still out there, fighting finals. In the round of 16, and the semis, always giving it a shot. He gives his all, both emotionally and physically. His eyes burn with desire. He is my type of player.

Sugar Ray Leonard. This guy made punches almost poetic.

Once I saw him fight Thomas Hearns. Sadly, only once. Lots of sportspeople admire fighters for the reason the great Joe Louis stated — because boxers can run but they can't hide.

In team sports, much of the time the guys not making the effort can hide.

Not in boxing, though.

Sugar Ray, such a great mover. So skilful. And what about the way he finished them off. Goodnight, Irene.

Michael Jordan.

I couldn't even qualify his greatness, having come no closer to basketball than the nextdoor neighbour's hoop, but the records indicate he goes considerably well.

Writes OK, too. I have been fortunate enough to read a couple of his articles. Not just read them, but obtain inspiration from them.

In fact, just last year I bought 20 of his books, one for each of the first graders. It was only a little book but contained some of the best messages I have ever read.

Titled *Michael Jordan in Pursuit of Excellence* and sub-headed *I can't accept not trying*, it not only explained his championship on-court qualities but his greatness off it.

The bit on the back cover reads: "I can accept failure, everyone fails at something. But I can't accept not trying."

Excellent. Linford Christie, I'd pay a fair bit of money to go and see Linford Christie, even if it wasn't for long.

Here's a guy at an age where he's not supposed to be running those times, yet he's getting faster.

And faster. Again, it indicates to me great commitment to being the best he can be.

So many guys want the scrapbooks, the accolades, but they are not prepared to make the commitment.

And Kieren Perkins.

I admire him not so much for what he has achieved in a sense of records but because he's an average guy from Brisbane who keeps lifting when it really matters.

He reached the top so quickly, battled the stardom and commercialism, but came back better, faster and more determined.

After his great success at the Commonwealth Games in Victoria, Canada, a friend asked Kieren whether he wanted a beer? "Love one," he said, "but I'll wait until after Rome."

The World Championships were three weeks away but it was obviously worth the wait.

With guys like Kieren Perkins on the team, you win.

And then you win some more.

Guys like him make all spectators happy. Coaches included.

BOB THE KELPIE RESCUES COACH

SEPTEMBER 10, 1994

Sheep are cute. Sheep are beaut. Sheep are soft and curly. But when I take them into town, I have to set off early. 'Cause they never go the way I want, so I need someone to help me. I just give a whistle, and call for Bob the Kelpie.

Don Spencer's song, *Bob the Kelpie*, is my son's current favourite.

This I know because between the time Steve Renouf was cited on Monday and cleared on Thursday night he played it, top to bottom, precisely 549 times.

I'm at training with quite a serious mob preparing for a sudden-death semi-final and in grave danger of bursting into song about cute, beaut, soft and curly sheep and a dog named Bob.

And this, of course, was not the Broncos' lone concern this week.

Look, I didn't take a real lot of notice of the tackle, not at the time. I remember Steve Renouf coming at Jack Elsegood at great speed, skidding, his body peeling off to one side at the last minute.

Out of the corner of my eye I saw it flash up on the big screen. I turned to watch it again, quite comfortable in the knowledge knees in the back are not the go of Steve Renouf.

It wasn't until after the game, during the press bit in the corridors under the stadium, that I thought of it again.

A couple of journos were probing about it, and I thought:

"Here we go again . . ."

I went straight back into the rooms, straight to Steve, and asked him about the tackle.

"I didn't mean to hurt him," he said, adding that he didn't think there was much in it, definitely nothing to worry about.

I said: "That's fine. If you did nothing wrong, we've got nothing to worry about."

Next morning the papers led on the tackle and I thought, oh yeah, pretty typical.

But then the bells went off like the whole city was on fire.

The league general manager John Quayle rang John Ribot, our chief executive, to inform him Steve Renouf had been put on notice for a possible citing.

We had never received a call like that from Phillip Street, never heard of anyone being put on notice.

So Ribot rang Frank Stanton, his counterpart at Manly, and Stanton said he hadn't viewed the tapes nor spoken to coach Bob Fulton about the tackle.

By the time I got to training Steve had been cited.

He looked relaxed, and I was, too.

So I just said: "Gotta go down, eh mate?"

He said: "Yeah, I've got no control over that."

Again he explained the tackle to me, "instinctive" being one of the words he used.

At our place, there's always plenty of geeing up, and one of the half-dozen of our guys to have been cited and subsequently suspended earlier in the year, said: "You're gone."

Another said: "Three months!"

Renouf said he didn't care whether he copped three weeks

> **"That's fine. If you did nothing wrong, we've got nothing to worry about."**

or three months, that he knew he had done nothing wrong and that was all that mattered to him.

We had a team meeting where I told them I thought Steve would be cleared, that we could not allow it to affect our preparation for today's match against North Sydney.

At training on Tuesday I again grabbed Steve to ask him how he felt. Relaxed, he said, and I told him to keep it going that way.

On Wednesday we had a meeting for an hour and a half with our solicitors, just tying it all up, and then the word came through about the prominent football guy walking around Sydney saying, no, explaining, Steve was going to get three or four weeks.

We'd heard those things in the past, the daddy of them all being the highly respected journalist — ho hum — turned Nostradamus who not only told me what charge Kerrod Walters would be found guilty of, but exactly how long he would be suspended.

That guy is right on every occasion.

I did what I always do in these situations — headed bush, straight to my mate's farm with my son, the *Bob the Kelpie* tape blaring away.

We were sitting down to dinner before leaving for home and through 7.30pm and 8 o'clock when the phone rang a few times, my mate would say: "That'll be the news on Steve."

I told him I didn't want to hear it, that my way is to lock it out. I'd prepared myself. Hancock was going to be in the centres, Morris on the wing.

Anyway, the calls had nothing to do with Steve and we set off on the 90-minute drive.

Cane me for being corny, but I've always believed in this country, the fact that in the end honesty prevails.

My son Justin's listening to the tape and I'm thinking of my last words to Steve: "You've got to go in there prepared to lose, because if you go in in that position, then you can't lose."

And a tick before nine, and after a considerable debate on the pros and cons of survival without *Bob the Kelpie* for just a couple of minutes, I convinced my son to pop the tape and switch on the news.

It led the bulletin — Steve Renouf cleared!

I pulled up and gave my son a big hug.

He appreciated it, even though he didn't understand what it was for, and moments later as he sat back and started humming to the music again I wound down the window and started barking and whistling to the bush.

I felt a bit emotional, which is not something I easily admit. Cane me for being corny, but I've always believed in this country, the fact that in the end honesty prevails. For the remainder of the drive I reflected on a season of ups and downs, of tremendous adversity at different times . . . the hard decisions.

What I came up with was the quality of the young men with whom I work, young men with an ability in most cases of accepting responsibility for what they are and what they represent.

All week Renouf had looked at himself, and, like the rest of us, liked what he saw.

People underrate the effects on an individual of such things as public citings.

Just recently I was talking to a group of schoolchildren and telling them before they did something silly, to think how it would affect others.

One said: "Yeah, but if I do something silly, I'm the one who gets punished."

I suggested he have a think about that, about his mum and his aunties and uncles, that maybe in certain cases others were left to carry the scars.

It's true. Renouf is important to the Broncos, as everyone reminded us during our finals run last September.

First of all we couldn't win, they said, without Glenn Lazarus, then we couldn't win without Renouf.

We didn't have Renouf for Manly, and we didn't have Lazarus, Terry Matterson or Renouf for Canberra, just as we didn't have Lazarus or Matterson for Canterbury.

But we still won.

And that is a big part of the reasoning why I think sheep are cute.

Success can
sometimes mean failure

July 22, 1995

A man's treatment of money is the most desirable test of his character. How he makes it, and how he spends it.

At the moment there's a bit of money, more than a bit, around sports, so let's try to add up a few of the misconceptions.

Just the other day I read where Andy Haden, the former All Black turned players' agent, said we must realise that the game of rugby now belonged to the players and the fans.

But he was wrong on one count.

The games — and I stress *games* — now belong to the players and the corporations.

Where does the fan sit? In the stands. He has no control any more. A stranger who happens to read this column walked up to me and said a pretty sensible thing, how the fan lost control the day his or her admission outlay no longer covered the wages of the players.

The Australian Football League has done a survey on this very topic, and according to them the guy in the corporate box is already greatly subsidising the bloke in the beanie downstairs. It costs the average fan $11.60 to get into the Aussie Rules, whereas it costs the game $26 to have him there.

Money, to me, is not the problem in sports.

Already we have seen amateurism, whether it be the Olympic Games or world championships, take your pick of the track and field meets, cycling, go the way of the dollar.

28

Great professionals such as cyclist Phil Anderson are even competing at Commonwealth Games and we're seeing dramatic change in rugby union where their whole motto rode on playing the game for the love of it, that and for their team-mates. Money had nothing to do with it. It has all changed now, though.

The problem we face is how to handle it, both individually and as groups because success has made failures of many people.

In AFL and rugby league, where there have been fair incomes for a number of years, we have some experience in handling the financial situation but in rugby, well, the code is in for some difficult times.

I look overseas, to American football, ice hockey, basketball and soccer, and no matter the mountains of cash they still produce champions and high standards of play.

People say choose a job you love, and you'll never have to work a day in your life. I'm with those people.

And I don't believe players in the future will falter because of huge incomes.

Still, the pioneer has the mountain to climb, and then everyone gets to ride the lift. It might take two months, maybe three years, but there will be a time of adjustment in rugby.

The two major problems with money . . . greed runs first by a mile. Look at basketball and ice hockey in North America, the strikes about their pays, and remember they're not striking about the first million dollars but the fifth and sixth they want to make a season.

> **People say choose a job you love, and you'll never have to work a day in your life. I'm with those people.**

The second part? The fan. They're the people you don't want to alienate. While he or she might not be paying the total bill I would hate to go to any contest where there is no-one in the stands except for the corporate boxes.

Fans create the atmosphere so important to players. You could argue horseracing continues to prosper financially despite the fact the stands are empty but while the horses undoubtedly prefer the peace and quiet I'm sure the jockeys don't.

More than ever I sense the fan doesn't resent what the athlete is paid so long as he or she is not taken for granted. The fan smells greed a long way off, and if the wages go up and the performances go down — that's what they resent.

The risk in team sports is the guy who plays one year too many just for the money, the pay packet. He's out there hiding, getting so much and giving so little.

Ask someone who is sick what they most value, and every time they will say their health. Money never gets a mention.

I remember Paul Hogan during the Los Angeles earthquakes, saying how he could just pray he would be OK, that all the money he had accumulated could not get him out of those ones.

Always competitors must endeavour to maintain the attitudes that made them play the games in the first place: the enjoyment, the dedication, tenacity and perseverance that made them stars.

The money comes along only as a reward. If the competitor becomes complacent, or satisfied, as a result it's goodnight from him and good night from you, money being a terrible master but an excellent servant.

> **Always competitors must endeavour to maintain . . . the enjoyment, the dedication, tenacity and perseverance that made them stars.**

In my playing days — and this is something I have forbidden as a coach — it was not rare for a well-heeled supporter to come into the rooms before a big match and offer us $500 a head to win.

The team would invariably go out and play terribly. I realised then, and still do, money is not the main motivation in sport because if it was we would have won those games.

It's only important when you sign the contract, when you are doing the deal, but when that's over it should not matter and with the great majority it does not matter.

For the past couple of years at the Broncos we have had a boy, well short of his 20s, who has just had an offer of a huge amount of money from a rival organisation.

In a conversation with our general manager and others I decided we would not even make him a counter-offer but instead let him go. He's gone. The story here, I just felt if he stayed at our club he would be staying for the wrong reasons.

I also believe, at such a young age, he should be worrying about where he's going instead of arriving somewhere — and if he's going to go to the highest bidder now, he's most definitely going to go there a few years down the track anyway.

I'll tell you what I worry about in regard to money and sport.

I worry about the guy you need in the team, the guy who is not a super star, yet his contribution is just as great. You know the super star, he's always going to be courted but not the guy who might have missed out on a bit of grace but no grit.

One thing you cannot coach against is the fact that some of them will finish their playing careers with nothing to show for it except their scrapbooks. They make poor business decisions, waste enormously, but there's nothing you can do about it and I find that very frustrating.

There are two ways to get enough. One is to accumulate more and more, and the other is to desire less.

wayne BENNETT

ON VIRTUES

*None of us know how much
is inside until we are faced with an
extreme situation.*

HEROISM HAS NOTHING TO DO WITH LOYALTY

APRIL 22, 1995

This word loyalty keeps appearing every day in my life and I try to put it all into perspective.
The Australian Rugby League uses it continually . . . if a player is going to put his future in the hands of the establishment he signs a *loyalty* agreement.

I'm sure we all know the meaning of loyalty, or at least think we do, and I doubt there's anything more daunting than when someone accuses you of disloyalty.

The question I ask is: Loyalty to what? In some cases, the person questioning your loyalty has tried to buy it.

Not so much in a financial sense but he has done you favours and given opportunities, shown you a path to follow.

Yet down the track the same guy jumps up and says: "Hang on, you can't take up that opportunity, follow that path . . . because if you do you're showing no loyalty to me."

I've certainly been in a lot of situations at the Broncos where a player is contemplating a richer offer from another club.

The common rebuke: What a jerk, this guy has no loyalty to our club — we gave him money when we shouldn't have, we found him a job, a house . . . you know, I have never seen it that way.

When you do someone a favour, help them to be better than what they are, you do it for one reason: because you want to.

If you do it because you're looking to buy loyalty, get out of here. All you can hope is that the person will appreciate what you have done.

I would tend to think that if somebody leaves your club they are not being disloyal, that loyalty has little to do with it.

Most of the time they have appreciated everything that has been done for them and they know, as I know, the buying of loyalty was never part of the deal.

> **When you do someone a favour, help them to be better than what they are, you do it for one reason: because you want to.**

The club shall remain nameless but once I took a coaching job and, as always has been my habit, the first thing I did was approach the senior players to ask about the shortcomings of the joint.

To a man, they named one member of the staff, deeming him inadequate.

So I had to make a change, and swiftly, and went to the chairman saying so and so has to go.

He said: "No way, he's been loyal to me and I'm loyal to him."

What? I said that's great, but the guy can't do his job properly, doesn't have the confidence of anyone. This is where loyalty gets dangerous, impractical. It's blind loyalty and even the chairman agreed, when pushed, that the guy couldn't fire.

One of the greatest improvements in rugby league over the past decade has been the quality of coaching and coaches. And I know why: because they've been made accountable.

Besides the player, the coach is now the most accountable person in a club.

When he gets the sack, you hear the cry: "This joint has no loyalty."

Craig Young at St George, the guy played a lifetime there. Next day he's appointed coach and then, bang, he's sacked. Bye Craig.

Alan Thompson at Manly. He played a lifetime there before one day being rewarded with the first grade coaching job. Bye Alan.

Mark Murray at Easts, they didn't even let him see out the season.

Steve Martin at Norths. The Bears hadn't won a premiership since the Ice Age before Martin won them one with reserve grade.

You got it, they sacked him, too.

Frank Curry at Souths, he slept in red and green pyjamas. Bye Frank.

I'm not saying any of these clubs were wrong but you can't talk about loyalty and not practise it.

What happens is they make a business decision they believe to be in the best interests of the club and I have no qualms with that. But be loyal only to performance. When we employ somebody, we buy their services *not* their loyalty.

Loyalty, I see it as being relevant to my family and friends but I'm not employing them and I don't expect the same from them. With them I'm not trying to run a business . . . If I was I'd treat them entirely differently.

After eight years at the Broncos my use-by date is coming and sometimes — not often, but at times — I wonder whether they are going to do a Tom Landry on me.

Tom Landry coached the Dallas Cowboys for 27 years. The club got a new owner in Jerry Jones who celebrated his acquisition by sacking Landry.

The whole of America erupted in debates about loyalty, but when my time comes I will never say the Broncos were disloyal to me just because I gave them all those years and they fired me.

> **Be loyal only to performance. When we employ somebody, we buy their services *not* their loyalty.**

The reality is, I'm going to go and rightfully so. Not today, but some day.

I just hope I see it without them having to tell me.

Who am I loyal to? Rugby league. It has given me everything and I feel a kind of responsibility to help make it a better product.

Like me, you've probably heard the comments that one of the saddest things about the Super League-establishment battle has been the demands on the kids, some as young as 12, to sign loyalty agreements. No-one is more conscious of children than I.

I see their eyes when their heroes run by, but I rest fairly easily in the knowledge these kids live in the real world.

They have been sitting there when their dads have come home redundant, just as they've been there when one of the parents has changed jobs believing it to be in the best interests of the family.

And I know that they know and I know that Allan Langer, Ian Roberts and Laurie Daley are no lesser people for making a decision to ride their futures in another competition.

One day, these young guys will have to make a hard decision and if the poise and dignity displayed by the Langers and Roberts and Daleys over the past month helps them just a bit, that's great. That's what being a hero is about. Nothing to do with loyalty.

Honesty Plus Ego Spells Teamwork

April 30, 1994

A lot of people preach teamwork but practise mistrust and selfishness.

In teamwork — the leader, whether it be the coach or the captain or the army guy with whatever ranking — the most significant part is that he practises it too.

The old adage about a champion team always beating a team of champions says a lot but it doesn't say it all. For one, there's nothing in there about how to build a team.

Wherever there's a group of people involved the first thing is to all work together, get on, in the understanding that the team overrides the individual.

No-one will ever jump up, say: "I'm bigger than the team." Still, you're always looking at their actions.

The guy who believes he can't be done without, who figures he should be the centre of attention, who's selfish or full of himself, he's the one who ignites power struggles. In power struggles, people take sides. No-one wins. So at the first opportunity you move to eliminate the problem.

It's about ego. There's nothing wrong with ego so long as it's healthy, one which promotes confidence but still allows its owner to be part of the team, one which promotes leadership even without the captaincy yet realises the owner is not indispensable.

One guy full of himself, and the team's in trouble. Two or three? You're no chance, particularly if the guys have high profiles, commanding a fair bit of respect outside the game.

He won't share. At halftime, when he knows his mate's tired but he still can't pick up a drink for him on the way through. He gets asked for a lift, knows it's out of his way, says: "No, I gotta get home — see ya."

The little things, they erode away at the team.

Honesty, that's the other thing they must have. One of the great sayings the Americans came up with is: "I goofed." I made a mistake, in other words. Players — anyone in a group situation — if they can't say that, they are without honesty.

They need common goals, week-to-week objectives and the realisation when the team has success they all get rewarded.

Teamwork can't happen overnight, it has to be developed, built in time. When the Broncos came together in '88 we had a lot of great players but we were lacking.

In their second year, the Adelaide Crows coach, I read somewhere, took his players away and one of the things they did was walk over hot coals. One of the players got his feet burnt, and I remember the criticism at the time.

I knew what he was trying to do. At the Broncos we haven't done the hot coals bit but we have been to army camps, put in horrible situations of adversity and found out who wouldn't carry the drinks at halftime, offer the lift and seek the soft option.

John Kennedy, the great Hawthorn and North Melbourne coach, once said: "In the faces of the greatest adversities the game can promote, each and every member of the team must know he can depend on each and every one of his team-mates not to let him or the team down."

> **Teamwork can't happen overnight, it has to be developed, built in time.**

I've had some tremendous experiences in my coaching career epitomising the making of a team. In the Brisbane competition in 1985 we'd been through some tremendous adversity and, six weeks from the end, were playing at Redcliffe in a match that would have a major bearing on the semi-finals. We put them away late in the game. It was such a tough match, awesome, and when it finished I knew we'd win the grand final.

They knew it too, more importantly. I still remember the day. I said: "You're going to win the grand final." They just looked at me, too tired to talk.

Same with the Broncos a few matches from the end in 1992. A cold Friday night out at Penrith, one hell of a football game. It was not spectacular, just tough and we got up on the bell. I told them that night too, that they'd win the grand final. We had been five years building. When someone was down, another would put in.

At different times the team will struggle and often someone will say: "Let's go out and get on the drink." But I've never felt getting on the drink with team-mates builds too much spirit. It might not do a lot of harm, but it's not the answer. It solves nothing. Spirit is built out in the middle.

I try to avoid rules and I believe the perception to be that I have just two: I'm always right; and if I'm proved wrong, rule one still applies.

I have, in fact, three rules: be on time; when I'm talking, give me your attention; and train and play flat out.

Arrogance,
Thy Real Name is Confidence

May 25, 1996

Late in the just-completed cricket season, I heard Rodney Marsh on ABC Radio defending the Australian team against accusations of arrogance.

Many people are deemed arrogant. Some rightly, too. Away from the sporting fields, recently, look no further than our former political leaders Paul Keating and Wayne Goss.

In my opinion, none of the accused are arrogant people. What I saw in them — and what I see in most successful people — is confidence, just as I see a lack of confidence in those who never achieve their potential.

If you are good at something, anything, you have to be confident in yourself. At times, at the bottom of hills, we see trucks that won't and can't move. They remind me of people without confidence.

Arrogance is an easy thing to label someone with, particularly for those with no comprehension of confidence. To me, arrogance has several meanings, but basically, it's when you're good at what you do and you treat people — friends, workmates, fans — like objects. Like rubbish. They only matter when you're in the mood to give of yourself.

One of the things I've noticed with arrogant people is, when they're down a little on confidence, they need your friendship and support. They need encouragement. But when they're running with the wind: Hey, what's your name, fella?

40

Sure, I know a few football coaches who are arrogant, but I know many more coaches and players who are simply confident.

Hard to make the differentiation? No. You just watch the way they treat people, particularly those deemed less important. Even in the team structure. For all the Origin stars, the Allan Langers and Laurie Daleys and Glenn Lazaruses, there have to be the Alan Canns and Jamie Ainscoughs, and the latter are just as important as the former.

Muhammad Ali, as was his way, once said: "It's hard to be humble when you're as great as I am." That's probably the height of arrogance. Right? Maybe, but the only place I ever saw the great Ali as being arrogant was in the boxing ring.

> ## "It's hard to be humble when you're as great as I am."
> MUHAMMAD ALI

At times the Broncos have been described as arrogant. This I know about the Broncos — they're very confident in the way they go about playing football. That's why they and certain other teams, be it in the club, Origin or international arenas, put doubt in their opponents' minds, which is what they set out to do. Inner-arrogance, it's sometimes called.

Certain people are forever confident about their ability, and confidence is contagious, just as the lack of it also rubs off.

The other thing about a confident guy, when he comes off the field he just blends in. With his family, other players — suddenly, he's just part. An arrogant guy, he can't do that. Off the field he has to still give a performance when there is no need for one. He has to be on the stage. All of his sentences begin with "I" and he never has time to listen to anyone.

Joe Garagioloa was a Major League catcher and later broadcaster. This is what he had to say: "You're good, you know it. But you don't wear it on your sleeve. You don't have to tell everyone you've got it — they already know. If you start telling 'em, it usually ends up lip-service, anyway." Go Joe.

To be a star, and stay a star, you need a certain air of arrogance about you — confidence, a belief . . . body language on the field that says: "I can do this, and you can't stop me."

When the Broncos won back-to-back premierships, Glenn Lazarus used to say: "Let's go out and play with some arrogance." He said it a few times — publicly and privately — and I never felt comfortable with it.

So we sat down and had a talk, and agreed that while the word arrogance was being used the meaning had more to do with the confidence we had developed in ourselves and others.

Arrogance can be humiliating in every way. Confidence? It is a glorious celebration of life.

FOOTBALLING INSTINCT, A QUALITY YOU CAN'T TEACH

MARCH 19, 1994

It is a quality, a sense of honour no-one can coach.

In last week's opening round against Parramatta, Brett Plowman put a very good hit on our Peter Ryan.

Ryan lost the ball in the tackle — it really shook him up.

With the feed Parramatta won the scrum and Ryan, still hurting, made the first tackle.

Parramatta's second play went to Plowman, with Brett Galea first up in defence. Poor Brett Galea. Ryan just came storming through him to make what I consider to be the second-best tackle I've ever seen in football. (The same guy made the best ever in a reserve grade match against Illawarra a couple of seasons back.)

That's the quality — the player is stung, rattled but all he wants to do is square up. Totally legally. He wants to inflict the same amount of pain that has been inflicted on him, perhaps more.

In people, that's the character you like to see . . . they get a setback, get a knock and all they want to do is climb back, and that's one of the things that really excites me about football and footballers.

I've always loved watching big Mal (Meninga) play, the power and grace when he's got the footy.

Another Canberra player, (Noa) Nadruku, he excites me. When he runs, something's going to happen. It was the same with Michael O'Connor, so graceful. Brett Kenny, just the complete player to me. And Gene Miles, that ability to pass. He was always doing the unpredictable, Geno, a tremendous athlete.

The more I see the way a lot of coaches are coaching the more I'm convinced that outside of being a good athlete not much is required.

It worries me because I think we're getting to the stage where kids are over-coached. We're producing more guys capable of playing first grade but they're not passing, not taking risks and I don't think it's improving the standard of football.

Obviously a player still has to be able to catch the ball, but a lot of teams seem to go for the big and strong, with good mobility. He gets to the advantage line and invariably dies with the ball. They're yardage runners, they can tackle and they can get the job done.

An old coach up here in Brisbane, Bob Bax, a great coach, once said to me that if a guy comes in with a stats sheet that's all clean, he hasn't been doing much. He's been taking no risks. Assume he's tried nothing.

I like to see a bit of flair, the unpredictable, particularly when I first see a player, the ability to run and pass and take an option.

It might not always be the right option but he's got to be trying something.

Don't get me wrong, you don't want a side full of space cadets. If he's been in the Winfield Cup for a long time and is still taking too may risks, you're not going to refine him. But if he's a kid in the bush — he's the one you want.

> **The first few times you shave, when you're young and just growing up, it's a great thrill. But when it's every day, a bit of a chore, that's when attitude counts.**

To be a first-grader he has to be a good athlete, and even the small guys need super strength levels. He must have good speed, even the front-rower. It might not be how long it takes him to cover 100 metres, it might be 10 or 15 metres, the ability to move laterally, to play the ball quickly.

Then he has to be able to handle the grind.

The first few times you shave, when you're young and just growing up, it's a great thrill. But when it's every day, a bit of a chore, that's when attitude counts.

Two guys I brought here to the Broncos, they both thought they were ball players. One guy came to grips with if he did it the way we wanted, he'd play first grade. The other guy? He's some place else now.

Next season, with the spread of players because of the 20 clubs, there will be some positions filled by players not genuine first graders.

To be competitive and not too vulnerable the coach is going to have to program that player so much, minimising all risks, which, to me, doesn't improve the game.

I realise why the League wants to expand the competition, but the problem is having enough players to go around, the skill levels.

Even when a lowly-placed club unearths a star, he's going to get offers and trot off to one of the top clubs.

Already the trend is here.

FEAR CAN BE
MASTERED WHEN IT'S OUT IN THE OPEN

JULY 23, 1994

Courage, in rugby league, is not blindly overlooking fear, but seeing it and conquering it. It's a thing we seldom discuss as a team or in life itself.

But in body contact sports there is no doubt players require great courage.

Fear, or the inability to conquer it, is one of the major reasons many young men don't play body contact sport. And it is dangerous to body and limb.

Often you see analogies between war and sport when, in reality, they cannot be compared. In one there is the possibility of death. But, in sport, while there's injury, a combatant can get off if he or she wants, they can back off. Take their ball and go home.

Physical intimidation is a big part of our game, and it's true the fear factor is not often talked about. You'll hear the comment that that guy doesn't like body contact, or this guy's playing a bit scared when in fact all footballers are showing enormous courage just being there. It's just that certain others have their fear factor under greater control.

All players fear. In the changerooms you see the different signs, some guys dry-retching, other guys sitting in corners so apprehensively, yawning, their stomachs churning.

Once the ball's kicked off, though, and he gets knocked over, the worries usually pass unless it's a particularly bad start to a game, a confrontation, say, he loses, and then he'll take more time to adjust.

The worst part, the greatest challenge, is definitely the wait, whether it be in the dressing room or the trenches.

That's why after a game we sense so much self-satisfaction from those players who met the challenge, who overcame the fear. Still, the same contest is going to be there the next week, and the week after.

When I coached at Canberra, in '87 — and this was part of my development — I remember frowning upon myself for never having spoken to players about courage, let alone fear. Earlier, when I played, I felt I never had the courage of some others, and didn't consider myself as *tough* as they were in this department.

When I gave away playing, I finally talked about it and soon realised that in just playing the game I had passed the greatest test. I could have played other sports, but doing what I did each Sunday, tackling the fear, made me feel so alive. Worthwhile. If I hadn't met that challenge I would have lost self-esteem.

Anyway, at Canberra I realised some of the players had similar problems. I wanted to go to them but knew I wouldn't get the right response by tackling them individually — so I spoke to the team about my fears as a player.

We'd been down to Crookwell on a promotional session and were coming back in the night on a small bus. I told them how I'd felt weaker than others but that I walked away not looking down on myself, and when the bus stopped in Canberra there was this eerie silence as they all disappeared into the darkness.

If I hadn't met that challenge I would have lost self-esteem.

Within 24 hours I had one of the players come to see me personally, and another on the telephone. Both said: "You were talking about *me* last night, weren't you?"

I told them, yes, I had noticed certain things in their games. They just opened up and we talked about fear. Both were high profile first graders, and, thankfully, both went on to play a lot more first grade.

Ever since then I have made a point of openly discussing fear with players.

Just recently we had a young fellow here at the Broncos walk in and say: "Coach, I get scared out there."

I said: "Sit down, son — this is something I understand . . ."

Fear has nothing to do with size. The little guys weren't hiding behind the door when God handed out courage and just because a guy's big doesn't necessarily mean he performs as Captain Courageous. Hear the parents on the sidelines at the juniors, "Give it to the big bloke," "Go on, belt him — you're bigger than him."

Somehow, we take the confidence out of these big guys before they even start. It's so important not to question their courage, particularly when they are out there playing the game.

Fear has nothing to do with size.

None of us know how much is inside until faced with an extreme situation, and you're always hearing about and reading wonderful stories about parents saving their children, mates doing extraordinary things for mates.

So in football I have never underrated the value of mateship. See the great teams, it's true, they were great mates. They'd carry an injury for the bloke alongside them, carry on. The sides without mateship are the sides, often, without courage. Mark Twain said courage is the resistance of fear, the mastery of fear — not the absence of fear. And, as usual, he was right.

For myself, as I grow older, I think back to those clubs and players I have known and realise they have helped me to come to grips with my own thoughts on fear. I feel different about it to what I did 20 years ago because, then, I thought I had to have the absence of fear.

I mastered it.

DEFINING LOYALTY . . .
STILL THE HARDEST GAME IN TOWN

MARCH 26, 1994

The dictionary counts for squat when looking up the meaning of *loyalty* in modern rugby league.

Mark Geyer, Jacin Sinclair . . . and the Broncos certainly aren't removed from the dilemma with Trevor Gillmeister, one of our finest performers, now running around for Penrith.

As a young boy growing up, and when I played, loyalty was the dominant factor.

You played for a club, you were loyal to that club like the working people of the '60s and '70s who stayed in the one job. Their productivity might not have been great, but they'd been there for 30 years, in another 10 years they would retire and there was no way they'd change.

With the '80s and '90s, though, came major changes in the corporate world and sport was no different. Incomes exploded. Whereas the basic wage might have been $25,000, suddenly a footballer could earn $75,000 in a game he'd be playing anyway. Sometimes more.

Once, the guy who'd been a great player, who'd shown great loyalty to a club, when he wasn't at his top any more he stayed at the club, the coach, through loyalty, often keeping him in A grade. Not everything was driven by performance then.

Perhaps it was Aussie football's Ron Barassi who took the first big step. He'd been a legend at the Melbourne club for all those years, yet he went to Carlton. A giant step.

Slowly players changed their attitudes, too, to the point now where they come in with their managers, accountants and sometimes solicitors to negotiate contracts, the catch-cry being: "I'd like to stay, but if I get a better offer . . ."

In came the salary cap in rugby league and the draft in AFL and out went Trevor Gillmeister from our place and Gary Belcher from Canberra.

> **Blind loyalty is probably worse than no loyalty at all.**

So how do you define loyalty?

To Kelvin Giles, our club conditioner, loyalty is performance. When I speak to the players they say their loyalty is to their team-mates.

Mine? It is to the Broncos, to the organisation I'm working with. By the "organisation" I don't mean the board, the general manager or the players but in the best interests of everything and everyone.

Any decision I make must be in the best interests of the club. With Trevor Gillmeister last year, when I told him we couldn't afford him any more, he questioned my loyalty and it made me sit down for 24 hours and address the definition. I probably still have to address it within myself.

At Canberra in '87, when I was working with Don Furner, we had another guy on the staff who just wasn't right. Everybody knew he wasn't right but Don had this tremendous loyalty to him. We talked about that. Don couldn't make the decision because of his tremendous loyalty so I took it on myself to resolve the thing.

It was then I realised blind loyalty is probably worse than no loyalty at all.

Trevor Gillmeister filled Kelvin Giles' definition because he was a great performer, and Trevor was a loyal person himself. I told the team he had questioned my loyalty and he was sitting there with them. I told them I had to make the decision that was right for the club. Had we kept him, within two years Gilly would have been finished and in the meantime three other young forwards would have been lost to the club because of the cap.

I made the decision for those reasons, as much as it hurt me, and there's still a lot of sentiment regarding that particular guy. I'd had to do it before, though not with such a prominent player — and I know I'll have to do it again.

Still, my loyalty to Trevor Gillmeister and a lot of other people is the same it's ever been.

Peter Jackson. I had him in the Brisbane club scene, at Canberra as well and while things didn't work out with him at the Broncos, we still have a great relationship and I still regard him as a friend. There was disappointment, but there was no blind loyalty.

I see Mark Geyer and Jacin Sinclair come up, being released from Balmain two games into the season. No criticism of Balmain — they're the only ones who know the facts — but if you have a contract with a club it must be fulfilled under most circumstances.

If a player's not doing the job, there's always reserve grade and there's the bench for reserve grade.

A contract's a bit like a marriage. It's easy to walk when everything does not go to script. At the end of the season, when both parties have done everything they can do to honour their contracts and it's still not working — that's different.

In days gone by, the player played footy and the coach coached.

Now there's the income, the manager who runs off at the mouth when he doesn't have to go out there and back it up. It's not what I tell the player or what his wife tells him, it's the bloke on the 10 per cent.

A lot of the guys out there still have a good appreciation, don't worry, of loyalty.

But I know the fans are left to wonder.

Once I visited the great Liverpool soccer club in England and remember asking their manager Kenny Dalglish: "How do you handle the expectation?" Dalglish paused, before replying: "That's for the fans. Our job here is to perform as footballers — we're footballers, nothing else."

I really don't know whether or not that is relevant here but I do know the Allan Langers will come and go, the Kevin Walters, and I'll come and go.

The fans, they get to hang around.

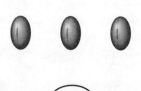

Lack of self-esteem a destructive element

September 2, 1995

Just this week I received a letter that made me think of a lot of things I had perhaps been taking for granted. Big things, too, like self-esteem.

The writer, a former footballer of considerable flair and gifts, told of how at different times in his life, his self-esteem had been so low he really couldn't appreciate the accolades and recognition.

Shoot me for taking self-esteem for granted. It's just that the lack of it is something from which I've never suffered.

But, sure, I see it in others. When you see or hear of a great talent wasted, if it's not through bad attitude the money's on it being through lack of self-esteem.

My understanding, or at least interpretation, of self-esteem is how you feel about you, and I remember somebody once saying no-one could make you feel inferior unless you wanted to.

The guy who can't handle a compliment, who's always looking for the ulterior motive to it, he's lacking, and in him I see elements of all human characteristics.

You sometimes want to grab him — shake him — and say: "Look, don't you understand all the wonderful qualities you possess?"

Look at the positives that make you, and stop dwelling on the things that, at day's end, mean and count for nothing.

Self-esteem, as I said, is how we feel about ourselves. Part of that feeling can be given to us by others: that's precisely why we have to be careful in choosing the people with whom we surround ourselves.

It's a question I often ask my younger players in particular: Who do you listen to?

Everybody gives so much advice to people in the spotlight, from social issues to finance and, of course, football.

While you can't stop that — and wouldn't want to — one of the things they have to get a grip on very early, is who to listen to and who to ever so politely ignore.

In the letter, the guy explained how his coach had told him certain things he knew to be right, but he instead listened to others contradicting what the coach had told him. Well, he made some bad decisions, didn't he?

Years later, in his own heart he realised the right and the wrong, and the bringers of both tidings.

The coach had told him: OK, he was a good footballer but he had to be patient . . . Others told him he was better than good already so, in Lord's name, why wasn't he playing in the top grade?

> **Look at the positives that make you, and stop dwelling on the things that, at day's end, mean and count for nothing.**

End result? He walked away from the game at age 20, kicking the ground instead of a football.

I've found, whether by accident or design, I can take advice from everybody but rarely will I use it, never unless it comes from an achiever.

By achiever, I don't necessarily mean someone who has scored a mountain of tries or kicked a few goals. I don't care what path they've gone down, so long as they've done the walking. That way, you know that they know the consequences — the price.

People who know those things rarely talk rubbish.

It's very easy to sound sensible. I know pubs and grandstands chock-full of people who sound sensible, but I only know them from a distance.

The writer made a lot of good points and one day I hope to

share more of his letter with you. Not now — now it's time for the playoffs.

Right now the big news in Brisbane, in the whole of Queensland, is that the Broncos play Canberra tonight at Suncorp Stadium.

In such times, no player is hard to motivate.

I looked it up — we haven't played Canberra in Brisbane since early 1993. What I didn't have to look up is the fact we have been subjected to some pretty hefty defeats on distant grounds in the meantime.

Canberra have had a wonderful season, losing only two games.

We had a severe loss of form during the season yet still lost only five matches.

When I say everybody enjoys these games I underrate the passion of the Walters family, with Kerrod and Kevin playing for the Broncos and Steve hooking for the Raiders.

Mum, we think, loves the Raiders and Dad, we're pretty sure, loves the Broncos.

Most importantly, both love their sons.

Through the week I said to Kevin: "Hey, it's going to be another tough night for your Mum and Dad." Kev just looked up, and his expression changed. Finally, he turned and said: "Never gets any easier for them."

You have to be careful what is said, because a wrong word to a player can do everlasting damage.

As brothers, the Walters have a great relationship. "You know, it's Steve's 30th birthday this week," Kevin said. Again he paused. "But I ain't ringing him," he said. "He can wait until after the game."

I liked that.

On any given day, these two teams can do what they want to any opposition and I believe tonight will come down to the outfit that wants to pay the price, both individually and as a team.

If both teams are prepared to pay the price, then it's going to be the contest everyone has hoped for — decided by a little luck or maybe a referee's decision.

Self-esteem will come into it, but only in the most positive of ways. You have to be careful what is said, because a wrong word to a player can do everlasting damage. At the Broncos this week, all the words and messages have been good. Talk is good. Action is better.

WINNING BREEDS CONFIDENCE, CONFIDENCE BREEDS WINNING

JUNE 10, 1996

"I never blame myself when I'm not hitting. I just blame the bat. And if it keeps up, I change the bat. I know that sounds silly but it keeps me from getting down in the dumps when I'm in a slump. It keeps my confidence up."

— YOGI BERRA, MAJOR LEAGUE BASEBALLER.

Just recently we were discussing loss of confidence, of performance, when a coaching friend said: "You don't know where it (confidence) comes from, or where it goes to."

So many talented players have failed to reach the heights because they did not have it. Confidence, that is. Yet, with it, I have seen just as many over-achieve.

Confident people realise their short-comings but, because of their confidence, work not just around them but with them to succeed.

It's about believing in yourself. How can others have confidence in you if you don't believe in yourself?

To players lacking a little on confidence I say: "Everytime I pick up in first grade, I'm giving you my confidence." In every player I have picked for first grade I have been confident even though some of them were not. They look at you. Sure, you can point them in the right direction, encourage them, but at days end it is not up to you.

Confidence can be shattered by injury, by failure, negative thoughts and by success. *Success?* With success comes other people's expectations and often the recipient begins to change things about themself.

When I came back to coaching in 1984 at Souths in Brisbane Mal Meninga certainly wasn't playing as well as I knew he could. He lacked confidence. Simple as that. His attitude was stilll great, he trained very well, yet everything Mal did on the field indicated he lacked confidence in himself. Soon I realised it was because he'd played State of Origin at age 19, made Kangaroo tours and goodness knows what. Suddenly, he couldn't climb over the expectation.

Throughout it all I remember saying to him: "When you were 18, and just kicking off in first grade, what were your expectations?"

Mal said that his only expectation was not to let himself down. "I never used to think very much about playing until match day," he said. So I asked him to go back to those simple goals, to the way it was and forget about everyone else. Everytime he got the ball, Mal Meninga didn't have to score. Nor did he have to save a try everytime they had the ball. Anyway, Mal went back to eating chicken sandwiches on match days and got through the next decade quite well.

Just the other day I spoke to one of my younger players who had just played Origin. He brought up the subject of other people's expectations and I went straight for the jugular. "I don't want to hear that again," I said, "and I'll tell you why . . ."

One thing we all have to do to help with confidence is learn to relax, don't ask too many questions. There is no special

> **One thing we all have to do to help with confidence is learn to relax, don't ask too many questions.**

psyche nor set formula to reaching our potential. Confidence is all between the ears — good and bad. Either you believe in yourself or you don't.

One of the characteristics coaches, managers, parents, businesspeople, whatever, fail to recognise is that the majority of people need time to develop confidence. You must be prepared to invest that time and recognise it in the individual.

Take Steve Renouf. The first time he played in the top grade he dropped so many balls. Later, I discovered his parents had come to watch him play and whenever his parents came to watch he dropped balls. So we had to work out how his parents could come to games and he could catch balls all at the same time. Happily, we did. It was a similar story with Steve's defence in that he didn't have the confidence to make the tackles he should have been making. With a little help, he built that confidence.

As people reach new heights they obviously grow in confidence.

About six months ago at a function I did something right out of character. This top sportsman, right, I'd followed his career and like everyone else knew he had been going through a tough time. I just grabbed him and said: "Look, I don't want to buy into your business, because I'm sure everyone is offering advice. Others even want to change your technique . . ." After a short conversation this guy assured me the only problem was an injury.

"Great," I said, "you'll be back on top soon." In his mind there was an obvious reason, you see, for the form slump — like Yogi Berra with the bat.

Never put doubts in their minds.

I look at Doug Walters, the former cricketer, and notice he is different in that he enjoys life more than most. He made it work for himself and I've seen great footballers who weren't great trainers and been very wary about tampering with what made them great in the first place. One of my favourite sayings is: Go back to what got you there — you're never going to be too far off the mark.

Go back to what got you there — you're never going to be too far off the mark.

Confident people don't need to fear failure. It has been suggested that confidence is developed by practice. Proper practice. Improper practice gives you nothing but false confidence.

Our players and our children and our associates, they all need good feedback and not someone always homing in on their imperfections. I'm really big into never putting yourself down on account of the fact others do that for free.

Some of the wise folk of sport have spent lifetimes wondering aloud about this subject.

Pro golfer Hubert Green said: "Winning breeds confidence, and confidence breeds winning." How true. If you don't believe in yourself, you're always looking for the negatives in others.

A quarterback in American football, some guy called Tittle, of all things, once said: "You have to have a past history of some success to give yourself status and self-confidence. You have to have accomplished something before you can believe in yourself."

And once that confidence is there, don't let others shatter it. Building it is a process, a long process. It's not like building a house, where you simply pick the bricks and timber. It's more complex because, as my coaching friend said at the very beginning, you don't know where it comes from and . . .

wayne
B E N N E T T

ON STATE OF ORIGIN

Origin football has become more like trench warfare, but the passion and enormous desire remains.

Pondering the Origin of Madness

May 21, 1994

As the weather cools about Origin time, I find the best way to warm the feet is to place them not in front of a log fire, but instead before a white-hot newspaper headline.

I can cop the State versus State, mate versus mate and even family versus family bit. Honestly, though, passions can border on the ridiculous.

For the best part of the week I've been in Armidale on the New England tablelands, where the mountain mists announce winter and feuds are not between the Martins and the McCoys, but between New South Welshmen and expatriate Queenslanders.

It's halfway along the back road between Sydney and Brisbane and newspapers are trucked in from both the north and the south.

One that I pick up screams: "Maroons blunder." And I think: Oh my God, what have we done? Shock. Horror. Reading on, it turns out Queensland have picked no ball-playing forwards.

So I look at the other team and I don't see any ball-playing forwards there either. I think about it a little further and realise there's only three ball-playing forwards in the competition these days. We've got one of them at the Broncos, Terry Matterson, and he's not playing on Monday night. Come to think of it, neither are the other two.

Again I relax, feet as warm as toast. Just as I'm feeling comfortable I pick up another paper and there it is: "Maroons not split."

Don't tell me my Broncos in the Queensland side have all been fighting — but reading a little further it's revealed that Tosser Turner has assured everybody they've never been more harmonious.

On the Broncos' final training night together our centre Chris Johns comes up and says, actually he kind of whispers it: "I'm really keen about playing for NSW, but Kevvie (Walters) and Alfie (Langer), they're just obsessed about playing for Queensland, aren't they coach?"

> **One of the big things for an Origin player is to keep his sanity — and the more he plays, the saner he becomes in this circus.**

I say: "Johnsie, it's been that way since they were born." Soon as NSW go into camp Kevvie will be on the phone, at dawn, telling Johnsie and Glenn Lazarus — our other guy born in the south — all the gory details about what Queensland are going to do to them.

One of the big things for an Origin player is to keep his sanity — and the more he plays, the saner he becomes in this circus. You'll see the first-timers going gaga, getting carried away. That's one of the reasons the selectors tend to stick with proven campaigners.

When the NSW team — chasing a series hat-trick — was announced it was obvious they had followed a Queensland tradition in rewarding those who had served them well. Loyalty can at times be fraught with danger but I can see the logic in it.

We were sitting together last Sunday night when the Blues side came through and, while excited for Lazo and Johnsie, a couple of my guys commented on different NSW players who are out of form but still got picked.

I made the point that by the faith and confidence the NSW selectors had shown in them, they had just said: "Look, no-one ever writes you a letter but the player is smart enough to realise he's back because of the way he performed last time. He knows what's expected. It's a tremendous motivation for him personally. He knows what he has to do to be picked again."

The only thing I'm not looking forward to about Monday night is seeing one of my players injured. Last year it was Steve Renouf, Chris Johns and Andrew Gee, his broken jaw forcing him out for two months.

I can understand the passion. Listening to the informed people of Armidale it's the women, you know, the *women* who want to see them fight. People not normally interested in football become very emotional. It changes people.

I met the craziest Maroon supporter, married with three children. The quietest little guy you've ever seen sitting there next to his wife, holding her hand.

She tells how she gets scared when Origin time comes around, the moment he struts into the loungeroom in his Maroon jumper and switches on the TV.

When Queensland score, he jumps up and tackles a bag he has strategically placed in the corner. A fight breaks out and he's into it, madly punching at shadows on the wall.

It gets to a crucial stage and he ups and throws himself backwards over the armchair.

I look at the guy — this nice, law-abiding citizen — and I say: "Is this true?" He looks at me sheepishly, pauses and replies: "I'm afraid it is, Mr Bennett."

SHEARER CLICKS IN
TO GIVE SERIES A ROWDY BOOST

June 17, 1996

Origin III, and you've got to be happy about that. We're almost through the 1996 series and the focus has rarely been on football, things like who's going to take the ball up or turn the match.

Maybe this time's different, though the build up has certainly had its lighter moments. For that alone, a big thanks to Dale Shearer.

No doubt he has been a tremendous player for Queensland over the years and even less doubt he likes playing for his state.

Some people thought it a bit cheeky on Monday, before the announcement of the side, Maroons' selector Arthur Beetson revealed that Rowdy — as we call Dale Shearer — had phoned him up. Big Arthur also made the point that Rowdy had not reversed the charges — again significant for those who know the veteran five-eighth.

When Rowdy was playing for me at the Broncos, whenever Origin approached he'd reveal how he'd just called Queensland manager Dick Turner or one of the selectors to remind them that he wouldn't let anyone down.

Rowdy's played a whole 10-odd games in three seasons — you'd have to check with him for the precise figure — but despite all of that he said when questioned this week on whether he was surprised to be called up for Origin III: "No, I thought they would have picked me for the first one."

Confidence is one thing he has never lacked. At the team medical Rowdy explained how he'd never missed a Queensland team medical even when he had not been picked. Why? "Just in case someone's injured or crook — I'm there, raring and ready to go."

During the week the Broncos were joking and laughing about it at training. We couldn't remember the year, '90 or '91 . . . anyway, Rowdy had played for Queensland but was overlooked in the Australian team. I think we played a club game on the Sunday and three or four of the Broncos, picked to play for Australia, were on a 6pm flight to Sydney for the national team medical. They get to Brisbane airport and you wouldn't want to know — there's Rowdy.

"What are you doing here?" they ask.

"Well," says Rowdy, "I'm coming down. You never know, I might be a shadow selection and someone might fail the medical. You just never know . . ."

Now, being the master of the gee-up, the players didn't know whether to take Rowdy seriously and when they reached the boarding part of Brisbane airport it was revealed he had no ticket, let alone boarding pass.

Not yet beaten, Rowdy approached airport staff and soon — to everyone's surprise — a passenger was off-loaded to make way for the "Australian" footballer.

So they arrive at the Australian team hotel on Coogee Beach, and Rowdy ain't there for the sunshine. The first person he runs into is coach Bob Fulton. Bozo's lucky, because he's coached Rowdy at Manly and knows what he's like. "What are you doing here?" he says.

"Well," says Rowdy again, "I thought there might have been a mistake with the team announcement . . ."

One of the Broncos standing nearby, who had seen Rowdy limp onto the plane in Brisbane and off it in Sydney, laughed before yelling: "But Rowdy, aren't you injured?"

"No way," he said, before tearing off down the hallway in an impromptu sprint-fitness test. So Bob Fulton gave him a bed and some Australian gear the next morning — then promptly sent him back to Brisbane.

He's a character, don't worry. This is the first time in Origin memory that he has turned up for a match and not been under a "fitness cloud". Like NSW's Benny Elias, he seemingly lived under those clouds for years.

Dale Shearer, for all the jokes, is an extremely talented and unpredictable player. No one is fitter than him. He's a closet-trainer, in that he does a lot of fitness work alone and cruises through the team sessions.

NSW coach Phil Gould has also been providing some comic relief. The one I'm still chuckling about was when he claimed referee David Manson got excited when Allan Langer scored.

I thought: Why wouldn't he get excited? I mean, David's a Queenslander and we all get excited when Allan Langer scores. Barry Gomersall definitely did.

Often Wally Lewis tells the story of Queensland being pinned for six tackles after six tackles on their try line, in a really tough situation, and calling to The Grasshopper: "Barry, we're going to need a hand here."

The other classic . . . it came on this really wet night, and Queensland had a drop-out under the sticks. The ball was so heavy Wally knew he couldn't get it out far enough with a drop-kick, so told prop Greg Dowling to distract Gomersall just as he was about to boot the ball.

> **No-one's immune from criticism, particularly in coaching, and the success of one year guarantees nothing the next.**

On queue, Dowling roared at the referee, who turned just as Wally punted the ball. Gomersall turned back to see the heavy ball sailing further and further downfield. He said to Lewis: "You got me, didn't you?" Lewis: "She'll be right, mate."

The only sad note on the Phil Gould matter is that David

Manson came out on the Monday and denied getting excited when Allan Langer scored. I just couldn't comprehend that.

Yet more comic relief, this time through the banning by Queensland of *Courier Mail* league chief Paul Malone. I read the article Malone wrote about Queensland coach Paul Vautin and thought it was a bit tongue-in-cheek. As far as baggings go in this coaching game, it was padded — lightweight.

Suddenly, *conspiracy* — Paul Malone and Wayne Bennett are working together to take the prized Queensland coaching job from poor old Paul Vautin. I think Fatty even intimated as much himself.

First off, Paul Vautin mustn't be feeling very confident in himself to worry about it in the first place. Then I got to thinking, how could Paul Malone and myself conspire to take the coaching job as the QRL have suggested? The funny part, to me, is that the QRL make the appointment. So, are they telling us that they are open to media manipulation? That coaches and players are picked by the media? Just wondering, fellas. Wondering and chuckling.

No-one's immune from criticism, particularly in coaching, and the success of one year guarantees nothing the next. Without doubt, one of my toughest years was '94 after we'd won back-to-back premierships. I can assure you it is not in my nature to do a coup, a job, on anybody.

The lesson for us all is you should never get too high on the euphoria of success nor too low on the drudgery of defeat. A balance must be kept.

Fatty's got to remember what Willie Pep, the old boxer, learned years ago: "First your legs go, then your friends."

WITHOUT PLAYERS THERE'S NO COACH

APRIL 15, 1995

It is only one month to the calendar day until the first State of Origin showdown of the year and it would be fair to say the series, and Queensland in particular, is in a bit of a mess.

I still don't know whether I'll be coaching Queensland.

This will be finalised on Tuesday when I attend a meeting with the QRL, but as I intimated to the directors 10 days ago: if all players, regardless of whether they have signed for Super League or the establishment, are not available I'll be resigning as coach.

When I went through the dilemma last December of deciding whether or not I would take the job the main reason I went down the road I did was because players from my club and others had asked me to, and it is ironic that now those same players are facing Origin bans.

At the time I first accepted the position, back in 1986, I was coaching director with the QRL, and in Rockhampton when Ross Livermore, who is still the boss, rang and said I'd been appointed Origin coach, I was elated, and outwardly so.

A decade later, when all the arrangements had been finalised for my return, I just kind of walked out of the office and drove home with no great outward excitement.

After a day or two of thinking about it, I kept asking myself why? And did I really want it for the wrong reasons, but I soon realised inwardly that the enthusiasm was there — it's just that now, being more experienced, battle hardened and sometimes battle weary — I have the same enthusiasm but it is a bit more concealed and, I suppose, a little more professional.

If on Tuesday I have to give it up it will be because of the major reason I took it on — the players.

In reverse, if the Super League people were telling me I could not coach the Queensland Origin team because I had signed with them, I'd quickly tell them to shove it.

There is a bit of the rebel in me, quite a bit. I'm OK if you leave me alone, but just tell me I "can't" do something, and I know it is legally and morally correct, I will try to do it to the nth degree.

I have spent a lifetime trying to do what people said I could not do.

Neither Super League nor Phillip Street has the right to destroy Origin.

A good friend from Sydney called the other day and said: "Queensland can't win this year's State of Origin."

I said: "Surely you don't mean that."

I know the task is going to be difficult, and again this call made me realise why I took on the job. If I thought Queensland were lay-down misères I probably wouldn't have done it.

Our Origin players have been coming to me, and watching me all the time.

A couple of the younger guys are particularly keen to play at this elite level and don't mind making it known but the seniors know I'm there fighting for them and have little to say about it.

> **There is a bit of the rebel in me, quite a bit. I'm OK if you leave me alone, but just tell me I "can't" do something . . . and I will try to do it to the nth degree.**

I've virtually banned Origin talk at Bronco training.

I don't want to denigrate the players who would be picked for Queensland if the Super League recruits were banned but I doubt even those guys would want to be part of a representative team which wasn't really representing anything at all. It's only when the politics are played that players taste real disappointment and get really dirty.

The other day I heard Arthur Beetson saying in an interview that if Queensland didn't pick the Super League players everyone would watch anyway.

But Arthur forgets that the last NSW v Queensland match before the Origin concept was played at Leichhardt Oval in front of family and friends. Today a ticket costs $50, and the best stadiums in the land, including the MCG, are packed.

Out of curiosity, sure, people would still turn on their TV sets for the first game and, especially the Queenslanders, they'd all be hoping for miracles . . . and being Queenslanders, the guys given the opportunity to play would produce better than their best.

But playing NSW is hard enough, and suicidal with your third- or fourth-best players. In the '70s, before Origin, NSW had no more commitment than Queensland, they just had better players, among them Queenslanders.

I know NSW are quite content with the players available through deals with the establishment and their coach, Phil Gould, is certainly close to Phillip Street right now.

The rumour mill has it, and I even heard Gould hint of it the other night, that while all players might in theory be available for Origin only a couple of Super League players will be picked.

That is simply not good enough. I have told the Queensland directors that, with just a month to go, they should have already decided on a replacement coach before Tuesday's meeting if it is not going to be fair dinkum selection.

I know that the Players' Association and News Ltd will back any barred players to the top of the legal mountain and everyone knows the League has Buckley's of stopping anyone from playing.

It's only when the politics are played that players taste real disappointment and get really dirty.

Look at cricket. Look at Tony Greig. When Greig joined Kerry Packer's World Series Cricket the establishment barred him from county cricket in England. But Greig played county cricket again, and soon.

It was the same with Kim Hughes here. When he went to South Africa, a rebel, they said he would never play for Western Australia again. But he did, of course.

So, the legal precedents are there but if State of Origin becomes a legal challenge I want no part of it.

It's like Phil Gould going around asking: "What will these players do if Origin falls over?"

Just go and play somewhere else, Phil. They'll hurt, but not as much as the fans.

GAME TURNED AT GIVE-WAY SIGNS

MAY 28, 1994

To my mum the "turning point" in football is when she gets to the intersection closest to ANZ Stadium, sticks her arm out the window and carefully steers the old Vauxhall hard right.

It has become one of the hip sayings of the modern game, the journalists sitting in the stands with the headline *Turning Point* awaiting them in the computer back at the office. The game was won the moment this happened or that happened — such wisdom. Every week everyone seems to know before me exactly where the games are won and lost.

Take Monday night and *that* try in the 79th minute of Origin I.

In rugby league terms it was a great try incorporating everything you want to coach. With the clock running down, the first thing Queensland did right was what they didn't do — panic. Instead of hoiking the ball madly from one side of the field to the other in search of a miracle they looked to two big forwards to go forward in quest of better field position.

More importantly, they waited for their backline to be set for one of those moments magically mirroring all those years of practice and drills.

Desperate yet controlled, Willie Carne knew his pass had to go over the top, and that he could throw it one-handed, on to Renouf whose juggling act with the ball we'd seen a thousand times in training at the Broncos.

With practice, there needs to be little or no thinking.

72

Thinking, with practice, transforms to instinct.

No way did Renouf have to think about catching that ball. He just caught it, like he had been practising.

Renouf and Michael Hancock haven't always been able to find one another, to link, and it had been a great frustration to me at times. Yet here they were in the single most desperate play of a desperate match, linking like brothers. Instinctively.

Renouf — Hancock — Darren Smith, they all drew their respective men before what was the critical part involving Langer, Meninga and Coyne.

Mark Coyne had been involved way back at the play-the-ball where Meninga was the dummy-half and Langer the first receiver and all they did was stay alive, heading straight downfield.

I thought Coyne did an absolutely remarkable job in getting the ball down. Here was a player totally aware of the situation, smothered by two defenders and caught short of the line.

Once I read an article headlined "Flow", about the mind being in total control of the body. I looked at Coyne as the fulltime sounded and thought: "Flow, Mark Coyne — and welcome to the magical moment of your life."

At night's end, though, it was not the only turning point in the match, the first coming at no single moment but for the

Thinking, with practice, transforms to instinct.

opening 25 minutes of Queensland's defence. NSW had scored on them and were coming back, cavalry style, trumpets and all, to score again and had Queensland not held out, they were gone.

The second turning point came with Carne's move to fullback when Julian O'Neill got hurt. With clever and daring positioning, Carne played the most vital role in Queensland's two late tries, the one for 12–10 by keeping the ball alive as he was going to ground, getting back to his feet and figuring again in the movement.

But perhaps it was a third turning point — unnoticed by most — that meant more than any of them. It had to do with NSW's elation at the Brad Mackay try for the 12–4 break. Every NSW player on the field, right through to the bench, acted like the crackers were going off on New Year's Eve. When I saw those

Blues jumping up and down on the bench, to me, that's just about the worst thing you can see in football.

Their actions stated: "Hey, we can't get beaten now."

A silly penalty, a dropped ball, a lack of desperation — they count the whole time through.

If I had been the NSW coach with a walkie-talkie I would have given them the biggest rev-up ever. No I wouldn't. I would have gone down to the bench, right along it, and anyone who jumped up I would have knocked down.

That kind of stuff is for after the game. When it happens during a game you know they are thinking: "We've got this, I'll just ease up, drop back a gear, make certain I make no mistakes and hallelujah, we can't lose."

The problem is your 12 other guys are saying the same things and suddenly everybody's focused on the outcome and not the next six tackles.

It's never the one thing that kills you. If you've done everything well from the kickoff you don't have to worry any more about the last 10 minutes than you did about the other seven brackets of 10.

A silly penalty, a dropped ball, a lack of desperation — they count the whole time through.

So that try might not have been the turning point but it was verification of Queensland's uncanny ability to create something from nothing under the greatest pressure.

It's what wins Origin, wins Tests and premierships.

Two points behind, two minutes on the clock, everything's riding and the players respond.

We don't just coach to see that, we live for it.

It is the basic reason little old ladies keep turning right into ANZ Stadium when they could just as easily go left in a dark cloud of smoke.

Club loyalty the Origin of success

June 25, 1994

Since Steve Mortimer's efforts in 1985, I consider the finest State of Origin level to belong to Benny Elias. His three matches for NSW this year were on par if not better than anything I've ever seen.

So a question arises, a question, as a coach, I'm most conscious of: Why doesn't Benny Elias — a range of players in fact — always play like that for his club?

The coach has no control, you see. It's the individual who makes the decisions.

Look again at Balmain, and while the performances of Paul Sironen and Tim Brasher were not quite the equal of Elias, they were still outstanding for NSW. On one hand Balmain's struggling yet three of their players are excelling at a said higher level of football.

Self-interest is often the greatest motivator, and Ben Elias, remember, copped much criticism when originally chosen to hook for the Blues ahead of Western Suburbs' Jim Serdaris. The coach has to wonder what Serdaris's form has been since he missed Origin.

At the Broncos I call it State of Origin blues — a player gets the media push, he's firing and really pumped up. Finally, the state team is picked, he misses out and his form suffers.

Significantly, in the seven years of the Broncos we have never lost a match on the eve of Origin I selection.

The club coach must do two things. First of all, make every player realise he has a responsibility to the club, to the people who pay his wages and gave him the opportunity in the first place.

Secondly, and finally, if that player will not realise, you quickly get rid of him. Straight out of the organisation. He's like a cancer — and his attitudes spread.

It's the most hollow of feelings, having half of your players off representing, doing what makes, for some, a successful year and the other half — back holding the place together — fall when the club doesn't make the playoffs. Individually some might think they've won anyway, but, to me, the important thing is how they perform week to week.

> **Self interest is often the greatest motivator.**

Today's column was to be totally different but after a telephone call to NSWRL general manager, John Quayle, well, it changed. John Quayle, I must say, has always been forthright with me and I learned that it was the Queensland Rugby League and no one at Phillip Street who decided not to proceed with action against Bradley Clyde for his tackle on Willie Carne on Monday night.

This, all players should know, was after the Queensland team management recommended that Clyde be cited.

Obviously, since its beginnings, Origin has had different rules to the rest of the football we know and play. She gets pretty cosy in there and I notice Steve Roach came out last week and confirmed that during his playing days for NSW he'd been given instructions, at different times, that he'd get away with certain things.

It just reinforced to me a happening in 1988 involving Blocker.

It came 10 or 15 minutes into Game Two, one of the hardest I have ever seen. Bob Lindner had tackled Steve Roach. Roach had played the ball, and it had gone from dummy-half through another two sets of hands when Blocker, with Lindner still at marker, just went whack and Bob fell to the ground. He received treatment and, later, stitches. It was blatant.

I remember very distinctly that for two days afterwards I did everything possible to get Steve Roach cited. I said to my players at the time that he had obviously been under different instructions, allowed to do what he liked and got away with it. For two days I hunted the media, the QRL, whatever, and nobody was interested. I was enormously filthy at the time and I still am.

Passion, desire, lies
— anything goes in this war

May 7, 1994

Three matches, all in a row. Three grand finals, so mentally and physically extracting. The expectation, the demands.

I remember coaching the winning Queensland side in the '87 series, the amount of people stopping me afterwards in the street saying how good it felt to be a Queenslander.

What a beautiful day it was.

There can be no doubt the sun shines brighter north of the border when the Maroons win the Origin.

The people, they just feel good about themselves, as if they played the games — were a part of it all.

I'd never experienced that until '87 and the only times I've since experienced it were when the Broncos won those comps.

I don't know whether or not it's the same in NSW and, you know, I really don't care.

Go watch the Queensland schoolboys play NSW, from under-eights through. I do. These kids in the trials, they're just kids playing footy the way they always do. Yet put them against the Blues and they're so emotional, pumped up. The kid who wouldn't normally fight – one spark, and there's fire.

No way is it just because they see their heroes doing it. It's partly because they always wanted to play for Queensland against New South Wales, the great state rivalry. They've listened to their dads since they could and they've heard the callers on the radio crying when Queensland's hit the front.

In 1967, at 18 years of age, I heard that guy who coined the phrase "It's great to be a Queenslander" . . . I was sitting at home in Warwick listening to him cry when Queensland won, crying during the call. Some people think it's corny, over-the-top. To me, it was magnificent, I loved it.

Three years later, representing Queensland Country against Brisbane, the old players like Ray Laird, Brian Fitzsimmons and Col Weiss, all Australian players, left you in no doubt what your sole purpose in life was: to make the Queensland team and face the enemy.

There can be no doubt the sun shines brighter north of the border when the Maroons win the Origin.

Johnny Lang, who's now coaching Cronulla, came along at the same time and he'll tell you too — it is life and death.

American coaches, in particular, carry on about life and death, and I can't understand. Sport is not about life and death. State of Origin is, though.

It's the ultimate sacrifice. It's the late Ron McAuliffe, a gentleman, walking into the dressing room and explaining your state has called you to do your duty. "And we expect you to do it," he would say. No surrender. Whatever the price, pay it. I remember Ron McAuliffe, the way he comes alive at State of Origin time. The tenseness, the checking, the pacing . . .

Seize and defeat.

Two of our Broncos, Glenn Lazarus and Chris Johns, play for NSW. It has not to do with personalities. Lazo and Johnsie are my great friends. It's just that Blue jersey. Once they put it on they really are faceless, I guess.

I despise the attitude if you haven't been to Sydney you really haven't made it. In sport or business. Sydney people have the ability to look down, maybe not even intentionally.

That's one of my greatest satisfactions — I never had to go to Sydney. I felt I didn't have to go to Sydney to get the brand on me.

After coaching Canberra in '87 I remember then, the reporters, asking me: "What did Sydney football teach you?"

Nothing.

In recent seasons Origin football has become more like trench warfare but the passion and enormous desire remains.

It's funny at the Broncos when it's over. When Queensland win Alfie (Langer) and Kevvie (Walters) can't wait for Lazo and Johnsie to arrive so they can really give it to them.

But when NSW win — and NSW have won the past two years — I try to gee Lazo and Johnsie up a bit, telling them to get into Alfie and Kevvie and the others. But they're a bit quiet . . . don't even go and look for the Queenslanders hiding in the showers and under the cars.

The media hype has become part of the series, the journalists themselves, they play their own game in the words they write leading up to the matches.

Administrators too. They get in their little boardrooms and pump themselves up, don't worry, wanting to be the dominant state.

The players, over the years some have risen tremendous levels as soon as they've pulled on a Maroon jumper. My brother-in-law, Greg Vievers, he'd get out and canter around in club football, yet when it came to versing NSW . . . like a draughthorse he'd virtually drag the Queensland team behind him.

As a Queenslander you just want to see them hold their position to the last man. To the last round.

Barry Muir was Queensland coach then and just as crazy in the stands, calling them (NSW) cockroaches and carrying on.

Wally, he just lifted when something was needed. I remember Paul Vautin one night when Queensland desperately needed a try, carrying three guys down the middle of the ruck for 20 yards when he shouldn't have got five.

Daryl Brohman. Here was a bloke who never made 25 tackles in a club game and the night I pulled him off with 10 minutes to go playing for Queensland he had 42 tackles next to his name.

Martin Bella, those charges. As the Broncos' coach now the only thing about Origin that worries me is I hate to see them injured, but I have no control. After the series they come home so tired but I know it's part of life. If I had a young fellow picked to do it for the first time I'd tell him to forget the hype and just do what he's been doing for the club . . . that nothing will be different.

Soon as he goes to the first Queensland team meeting, though, he'll know his coach has just lied to him.

As much as you want to be out there with them, you have no control and as a Queenslander you just want to see them hold their position to the last man.

To the last round.

How Vautin's Underdogs Became Top Dogs

May 20, 1995

In sport, as in life itself, the greatest inspiration is to be rated second-class and go out — head high — to prove everyone wrong.

Queensland coach Paul Vautin pulled a lot of right reins to get the Maroons home over NSW in Origin I.

The biggest rein he had no control over, however. It came on a platter: in Australia we call it the underdog mentality.

Monday night's events have been in the back of my mind all week because it was a classic exercise in sports psychology in that you can never underestimate, never brand someone second-rate, until the contest is done.

From time to time we all get knocked down. There's nothing special about being knocked down. It's the getting up we've got to cheer.

Queensland got up, and up again.

The thing that fascinates me is why we have to get bagged and criticised to get all psyched up for something special.

Then when the contest is over the references to its importance are never-ending — a contest that was not supposed to be a contest at all, remember.

The underdog form of motivation can be only short-term, but Paul Vautin would've been silly not to climb aboard on Monday and ride it until it dropped.

The athletes who stand above all others are the ones who fear criticism, the ones who refuse to take up positions of failure.

These are the great competitors, the winners, those who don't win once or for just one year, but forever.

Teams become great by being made up of these individuals.

Once I remember talking to Trevor Gillmeister. He'd been going through a lean period at the Broncos and I asked him for his opinion on what had made him so successful for so long? Trevor being Trevor, a guy who hasn't a lot to say, paused before replying: "I was not born to be a footballer, not physically, and definitely not a second-rower. They all said I couldn't do it, and that's why I did."

The underdog form of motivation can be only short-term.

This was in '93, the year after we'd won the premiership, and again I asked: "Could it be that you are contented now, happy with all the accolades?"

He admitted at the time that was probably true, and that's when I asked him never to forget what had made him a success — that fear of failure, and the critics.

It has become trendy to have 190cm, 100kg second-rowers but Trevor Gillmeister lives on in the Origin arena because of the little man's syndrome in wanting to prove everyone wrong, every week.

In proving that he must always be aware of the fine line between wanting to prove himself and having a chip on his shoulder.

Some guys take the proving to the nth degree and become bitter, so intent and intense they never stop to enjoy their successes.

Any fool can criticise, condemn and complain — and most fools do.

After just 20 minutes of Origin I the Queensland halfback Adrian Lam said he knew they were going to win.

I believe in that, I believe he knew.

Gavin Allen, the lone Bronco, said he knew almost from the kickoff.

Apparently, he was supposed to whack the Blues' Mark Carroll in the first scrum of the match but when he got there he didn't feel as if he needed to cause a commotion, that Queensland were doing just fine.

When young Ben Ikin was picked, from the clouds, his dad pulled him aside, saying: "Your body now belongs to Paul Vautin and Queensland — be happy with what you get back." I liked that.

Also special was the way Queensland destroyed NSW's game plan.

The Blues never planned or trained to play the way they did but, for Queensland, it went exactly to script, a script borrowed from American football, the scorched-earth policy.

They just went out and, defensively, burnt everything in front of them.

Paul Vautin showcased three past Origins before the game: the first-ever game; the third game of the series in '87, one of the finest ever played; and that match in Sydney in '89 where Bob Lindner smashed his leg, Alfie Langer his ankle and Mal Meninga a cheekbone but the troops still soldiered on.

> **Something I've learned, had to learn, is you can't always be the underdog. The more the success, the less of the dog.**

Just before kickoff I rang Chris Johns at home. He had a bit of an injury and I was just checking on him when, at the end of it, I asked how he thought the game would go?

And he called it great. He said: "Coach, NSW will have a lot of difficulty beating Queensland and I think Queensland will win by a couple of points. NSW will lack cohesion because they have so many new players."

When I got off the phone I just thought: "He's spot on, he's right."

One of sport's problems, and it's something I've learned, had to learn, is you can't always be the underdog. The more the success, the less of the dog. It's always harder to stay on top than getting there, and winning Origin I won't make it any easier for Queensland in Origin II.

If just one guy goes in with any less commitment, they're in trouble.

Adversity can be good for you, handled properly. What a night, with Ken Arthurson crashing through the media ruck to kiss Paul Vautin, a Queenslander — and a winning one too.

I read this just the other day. It belongs to an English author, and it goes: The child's philosophy is a true one. He does not despise the bubble because it bursts. He immediately sets to work to blow another one.

And that is what Queensland did.

"CONTROLLED AGGRESSION"
TALK A GEE-UP

JUNE 3, 1996

Often, when something is big — really big — we lose sight of what makes it so special and instead focus on images and impressions bordering on the ridiculous.

State of Origin II is, well, big, yet all week pretty much all we hear about is this thing, this image, called controlled aggression. In a matter of weeks we've gone from *Queenslander, Queenslander, Queenslander* to a bunch of "pansies".

Controlled aggression is what everyone in rugby league seeks but rarely finds and it's true that Origin I probably lacked bodies being put on the line, sacrifices in order to inflict as much pain on an opponent as possible in the eternal endeavour to make him lose the plot.

Remember, these are the finest players in the game and quite used to taking punishment.

One of the problems with aggression is when you start talking it up things can go awfully wrong, like your players getting over-excited where the intended controlled aggression surfaces as aggression not controlled.

That's one thing. Another problem is forewarning your opponent, allowing him to be on his guard. With the warning, he's more tense and ready to retaliate. Soon no one has control.

As Tommy Raudonikis said after the Wests–Penrith game: "We'll be ready for 'em next time."

Go no further back than last year's Origin II in Melbourne and

86

the very first scrum of the match. All week word had been out that there would be a brawl — at the very first scrum. Anyway, one of the NSW forwards got there and declared: "The first one of you bastards to call '*Queenslander*', we're going to bash." Story goes the whole Maroons' pack immediately chanted: "*Queenslander, Queenslander, Queenslander . . .*"

A few years back Benny Elias (NSW) and Steve Walters (QLD) were vying for the Australian No. 9 jumper. Steve was the incumbent national hooker and it all came down to Origin III with the Test team to be selected that same night. This fight started, and Benny ran straight for Steve. Just as the New South Welshman got near, though, the Queenslander cried: "Be careful where you throw those punches — I've got to play for Australia next week!" Benny? He just went crazier.

It reminded me of another fight involving Steve Walters, or, at least, almost involving him. I was coaching Canberra Raiders where Steve — or "Box", as we called him — was hooker. Against Canterbury Bulldogs it was, the first time Steve's brother Kevin ever played A Grade. This scrum broke up with Steve and Bulldogs prop Peter Tunks eye-balling one another, then shaping up with their firsts.

> **Controlled aggression is what everyone in rugby league seeks but rarely finds.**

Kevin, playing in the centres, was 15 metres from the action but I still remember hearing him call out: "Box, give it to him!"

Steve didn't respond, just remaining in the shape-up pose.

Again Kevin called: "Box, give it to him!"

But Steve still stood there, fists in the air but not moving.

Finally, and quite suddenly, Kevin came racing in with the words: "Bugger you, Box, I'll give it to him!"

Steve's at hooker for Queensland tonight and Kevin's on the bench. Neither were there for Origin I and should Steve start shaping up this time around I can imagine Kevin taking the bench on with him. Not just the players on the bench either, but the bench itself.

In my time as Queensland Origin coach there were some

terrible fights, particularly in the '85 season. The League were putting on that public face again, the code of conduct business, and I knew it was just another one of those dress-jobs they do because I'd seen enough to realise unless a player did something really silly he would never get cited.

So I refused to let Queensland management give the players a code of conduct. We agreed not to turn the other cheek. I said to the players: "If they (NSW) want to turn on the rubbish, don't walk away." Sure, I'd like to think we played with controlled aggression.

The problems with talking about it, pre-empting it, are the emotional levels out there in Origin. With the players wanting to please, they'll do anything and the talk has the potential to push them right over the top.

What disappoints me is that it's the players copping the hiding. The criticism. And the penalties. The lesser known or regarded player goes over the top and, bang, he cops two weeks. For what? Being a lesser light.

I suppose if any Queenslander has been put under pressure this week it is Andrew Gee because of the statements made by the coach. I recruited Andrew Gee when he was 16 years of age. He has had no other club coach. Andrew Gee is as tough a player as I've ever coached, and by that I don't mean Mike Tyson or street-fighter tough. I mean Weary Dunlop tough. Real tough.

It's an old tactic, distraction, and I think it might have worked in the old days. But only in the old days.

He has one desire in life: to please you . . . to do the right thing by his coach and his team-mates. He's a wonderful team guy and on a private level I have a very strong relationship with him. What's this all about? I just don't want to see him out there fighting, or being expected to fight, carrying on someone else's battles for them. Andrew Gee, tough as he is, has never been asked to do that for the Broncos, and he never will be.

So what's happening right here in the article is exactly what happens when the Queensland team is called a bunch of pansies —

*"If Alf has one major factor above everything else,
he's a poor loser. That, alone, almost makes us TWINS."*

"That guy — the No. 6 — he's pretty smart, isn't he?"

"Blocker Roach is a Blue always welcome in Queensland."

"Peter Sterling, he was the complete general,
in the Wally Lewis category."

"Never before or since have I seen a guy as committed to winning Origin as Steve Mortimer."

"Warren Ryan, the coach, alongside Jack Gibson, the most influential of the modern era."

"Matey," Peter Moore would say. "Matey, we'll sort it out."

"Fatty was funny as a player and those wisecracks you see and hear on the box are simply an extension of that."

"Whether or not Bob Fulton (above) and John Quayle want to admit it, the League raced around signing Australian and NSW players but totally forgot about Queensland and Origin."

"Phil Gould gets what he wants . . ."

"Brian Smith's a great competitor and really added something to rugby league in this country."

"I like what Jack Gibson stands for, the honesty bit and the team, the way he does things for people who can do nothing for him."

"My loyalty to Trevor Gillmeister is the same it's ever been."

"What I like most about the Broncos is their attitude to life, it's refreshing."

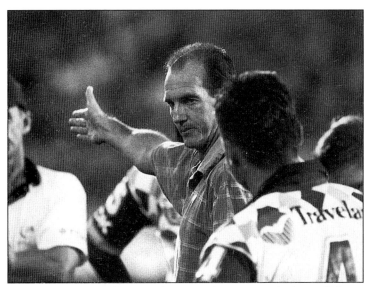

"The biggest mistake a coach can make is not to be himself."

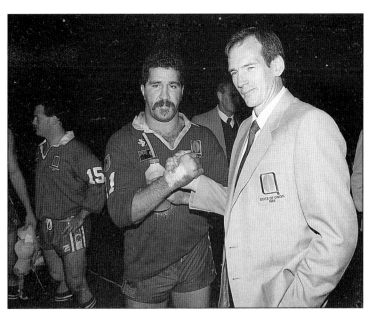

"The sides without mateship are the sides, often, without courage."

"I just like the way John Ribot never seeks a pat on the back. I like the way he handles adversity, his honesty, his consistency."

". . . Steve Renouf looked at himself, and, like the rest of us, liked what he saw."

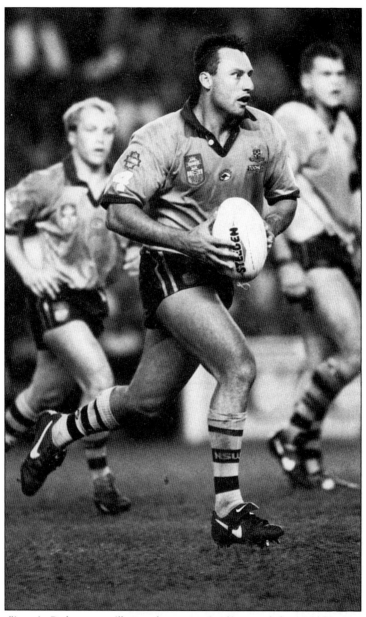

"Laurie Daley . . . will soon be recognised around the world, instead of just Australia."

"The greatest tribute a sportsperson can receive is the simple one of being a winner. Look at Mal Meninga's career, and marvel at a winner."

"Fred Daly, more than most, had a wonderful presence about him."

"When Allan Langer makes a decision, that's it. It's all over."

we've been distracted. It's an old tactic, distraction, and I think it might have worked in the old days. But only in the old days.

I've been trying to read between the lines and work out how much say Paul Vautin has in the Queensland team he coaches. With NSW, Phil Gould gets what he wants with a helping hand from Don Furner. That's the way it should be. I have no problems with that.

What gets me going about this? A journo got it right the other day when he said Queensland had picked a squad of 16, not 17 players by having *both* Adrian Lam and Kevin Walters on the bench.

I look at the Paul Vautin–Owen Cunningham relationship. Owen Cunningham plays at Manly and I know through discussions with Paul Vautin some time ago that the coach thinks very highly of the player. I do, too.

Cunningham does a wonderful job for Manly and appeals as an ideal interchange player at Origin level because he can play second-row, lock or hooker. His non-selection indicates to me that Paul Vautin might not be getting the team he wants, making his job much harder.

Every year Origin II is the toughest of the series because already there's a team one-up and two-up means no tomorrows. Queensland are facing a team in the groove, so confident in what they do.

NSW will be no different, the same methodical outfit which has won three of the four past series under Phil Gould's coaching. It works. Confidence, stability and belief make it happen.

Still, don't expect Queensland to throw in the towel. Even if someone throws it in, the rest of them will kick it back out again.

wayne
BENNETT

ON WINNING AND LOSING

Winners make commitments,
losers promises.

WINNING AT A PRICE

MARCH 25, 1995

Often I wonder what it is that brings one man success in life and mediocrity and failure to his brother.

The difference can't be in mental capacity; there isn't the difference in our mentalities indicated by the difference in performances.

In short, I've concluded some men succeed because they cheerfully pay the price of success. Others, though they may claim ambition and desire, are unwilling to pay that price.

These words, and others, were sent to me this week by a Broncos fan.

They originally belonged to Herbert F. De Bower, and they got me thinking.

Winners, I know, aren't born just as no-one is born a loser. It's what you make of yourself.

Something I always find fascinating is how sporting critics determine who is a winner and loser, because I don't necessarily agree you have to win all the time to be a winner.

Take the Pete Sampras–Jim Courier semi-final at the 1995 Australian Open, one of those great tennis games. Now, you couldn't say because Courier lost he's a loser. You look back through his career, at those marvellous statistics, and realise that no-one can be a winner unless they lose sometimes.

I love the one where the critic says: "He's a bad loser."

The player throws his racquet, his pool cue, kicks the hell out of the ground and storms off . . . I used to think he was simply a bad loser too, but as I grew older realised it was just a show for the fans.

The guy who mouths off in the dressingroom before a game is going to chicken out on you somewhere when the going gets hard.

In the United States I met Bill Parcells of the New England Patriots. They'd been losing for a long time before he arrived, and straight away he took them to the playoffs.

> **"You must take yourself wherever you want to go."**
> BILL PARCELLS

Parcells walked in and told them: "You must take yourself wherever you want to go."

The point is, if you're in a losing club or losing team, you have to be a part of the problem. What Parcells was saying is: you can't blame everyone else.

In life or football you either buy winners or you make them. By winners, I mean people like big John O'Neill, who played in eight grand finals for Souths and Manly between 1965–73. Wherever he went, he made winners.

People like Glenn Lazarus and Mal Meninga. Wherever they go they take an attitude, a winning one, and it pays off.

Take Wayne Harris, the Melbourne Cup-winning jockey. Through brain-tumour operations, brutal falls and weight problems, he just wouldn't give up.

All this is true in reverse, with certain groups and individuals who never win. There are people who make others play worse, who hold them back.

Manchester United, Liverpool, Herb Elliott . . . winning is a habit but, unfortunately, so is losing.

Anyone can have a bad trot but bad trots don't make losers, they just make you die a little. By keeping together a group that has had a fair bit of success, you've always got a chance.

The problem comes when you have a group that has never known or been associated with success. So when you get with the right people, you might not even notice the change in your habits, but it's happening.

Losing drives me mad, even if I don't show it. I don't throw pool cues, kick the family dog or go around beating anybody up, but I certainly retreat to the cave.

If I ever begin to accept losing, I'm out of the coaching caper.

At the Broncos I haven't mentioned the word "win" in season '95. It's not something we talk about. The anger and frustration you often see in "bad losers" is, in fact, directed at their own preparation, or lack of it.

I can live with being beaten and understand that if the team loses an individual can still feel OK in himself because he played well. I suppose a guy who doesn't play well but is in a winning team can feel good for the team, but I wouldn't, not if I hadn't made a contribution.

In our game winning starts on Monday, but for boxers with just four fights a year or swimmers who peak but twice a year, winning starts much earlier.

If swimmers stand on the blocks and know they cheated on a push-up or a lap three months beforehand, they're prepared to lose.

When a winner fails, he trains harder while a loser blames others. When a winner makes a mistake he says: "I was wrong." A loser says: "It wasn't my fault."

> **A winner feels responsible for more than his job. A loser says: "I only work here."**

Winners make commitments, losers promises. A winner feels responsible for more than his job. A loser says: "I only work here."

"There ought to be a better way to do it," says the winner. Loser says: "That's the way it's always been done here."

There is no greater tribute in sport than to be called a winner, especially when you've known the feeling of a loss.

After you've kicked the dog, it's time to face up to Sunday

June 24, 1995

Company general managers must have had weeks like this, facing a right royal public flogging.

Perhaps through business or family, you can somehow relate to the Broncos' week that was.

Last Sunday's performance against Illawarra was one of our most disappointing, and there was no indication it was coming before the match.

When I get home I have my own way of handling such disappointments, going into a cave where I say nothing, knowing words mean so little.

After a loss I don't normally go on but I did this time, telling the players of my disappointment in them, that there was no way they could possibly look one another in the eye and say they'd done their best. I looked up and 15 heads were down.

My wife, being perceptive, watches me get around the house head down in such weeks, mumbling, looking for the dog I don't own to kick. She says: "I couldn't do the job you do."

So I've had a week thinking about the job I do, in more detail than ever before.

My initial feeling was — I just don't want to do it any more. I don't want to go through this. Knowing my mood swings and feelings, that's quite normal.

My other tendency is to begin soul searching: Did I do a good enough job? Was it my fault entirely?

The only redeeming thing about Sundays like last Sunday is the night's sleep.

I hardly ever watch television these days but sat right through *Joseph*, a biblical story with some good messages. I wasn't looking for messages, just tiredness for a good night's sleep. It worked.

I woke up a lot more positive, still not feeling good but positive about what had to be done.

One thing I've learned in life is perseverance. Most importantly, you need to know where you're going, but secondly, you have to persevere.

So often we are so close to our objectives, only to walk away. Pioneers Burke and Wills died of thirst not knowing there was water over the very next hill.

At the time we think the hard thing is to walk away. We assure ourselves of that, but it's not. The hard thing is to stay, to persevere.

By Monday, I was in perseverance mode.

While the Broncos are still well-placed with a 9–3 record, we don't want to be turning up for the September playoffs as cannon fodder for the teams above.

Facing the videos on Monday is extremely difficult, knowing you're not going to see anything that hasn't beaten you before.

> **So often we are so close to our objectives, only to walk away.**

Then to team selections.

Last year when we struggled — and we haven't struggled so much this time around — I persevered too long with players because of reputations. That was perceived as a weakness, but we've been through so much together. With some players it's eight years, through all the highs and lows, and if there's any doubt you always want to give them the benefit.

Sure, you can adopt that *scorched-earth* policy and burn everyone and everything in front of you, but that's quick-fix stuff, not a long-term remedy.

You have relationships but I promised myself during the off-season if we ever went through this again I wouldn't be weak, I wouldn't make speeches — just take firm action.

If someone was a lair, or didn't train well or had a bad attitude, it would be easy to drop him.

But the people who make up the Broncos have no such traits, they're good people.

They don't go out to fail, and are guilty at times only of not preparing well enough for a match.

Monday afternoon's team meeting was not a pleasant experience, telling the players involved they wouldn't be in the first grade squad . . . no joy at all.

From 4.30 on Sunday until Tuesday morning we lived in our own little hell, but I'm starting to come out of the cave.

I realise it's important for me to be positive for the team. By positive I don't mean going around kidding ourselves, but at least looking forward to the next game. When I left that team meeting I said I didn't want to hear another word about Illawarra.

> **If you keep looking over your shoulder, it won't be long before you are going backwards.**

If you keep looking over your shoulder, it won't be long before you are going backwards.

Their enthusiasm's been good. Look, everyone has a theory about why the Broncos fail. Mainly it's to do with them being too well paid, being fat cats.

A guy once told me capitalists never make good footballers. If it's true, I hope dropping two players gets the point across, but if it doesn't I'm obviously going to have to look at that and bring some more kids into the place.

My farmer friend rang through the week, sounding more disappointed than me, and said just one thing: "Thinking about the ploughing doesn't get it done."

Losing is not the issue here, never has been. I've been around this game long enough to understand there has to be a loser, but no matter how long I'm around I'll never tolerate guys not giving their best.

Last Sunday I had four good players out of 15, but after the droppings and the kickings there was no backbiting, no signs of cancer, and no-one looking back.

This week we've built up again.

What fascinates me is that people can take a knock at work and everyone understands when they have trouble finding the motivation to go back to the office.

Everyone thinks footballers are different. They're wrong.

DON'T ASK ME, I'M ONLY THE COACH

SEPTEMBER 17, 1994

Even though there was only a point either way in it, the Broncos and Raiders fans are entitled to ask: What went wrong?

What a difference a point makes.

North Sydney score a deserved one-point victory over the Broncos and run away chock-full of confidence.

Canberra play in just as hard a game, if not a little more intense: extra-time, two shots at field goal bouncing back off the post to slap them in the face and, suddenly, unexpectedly, they have to front up again to play for a grand final berth.

Tomorrow's preliminary final combatants are both well coached. There'll be nothing greatly different in the tactics, just as both have individuals capable of performing the master strokes.

This, make no mistake, comes down to a battle of psych, a mind war to be fought to the tingling end of emotions.

The Bears have some advantages here. I certainly wasn't critical of their first semi loss to Canberra, thinking that, with a little extra luck throughout the afternoon, they could easily have won.

They then came out and knocked out the Broncos, a similar side to Canberra, and carry with them this extra motivation in the fact most people don't live as long as it has taken their club to reach a grand final.

When Norths arrived last Saturday to play us at the stadium our centre Chris Johns — and I'll never forget this — took one look at them walking in, turned to the others and said: "That's the look of a team on a mission."

There wasn't much I could say in reply. I can't do much about how other teams look but I do know how a player who is not feeling great can come into a group like that and turn around his feelings quite quickly.

Canberra? Everything had just fallen into place for them, but someone forgot to tell the Bulldogs they were supposed to be victims not victors.

That loss last weekend hurt Canberra, don't worry, physically but more so mentally.

The let-down won't come at kick off tomorrow but near the end of the first half, or somewhere in the second half, when it's 10–all or they are two points up, when the pressure's really on.

There will come a moment when someone who usually turns up for a big play won't be there, whether it be the diving on a loose ball or the charging down of a kick.

The missing guy, his body is going to be telling him: you've had enough, fella.

Canberra will start well as they always do but the test comes in psychological strength, that extra, undefined toughness.

Big Mal could be the key to it all. He's probably got to provide the inspiration for Canberra. Do something special when it is 10–all, make the difference.

At times like these a coach looks to the big-time player, sending him messages, generally relying on him. That is why that player gets the big money.

Just look at Alfie Langer last weekend, he was magnificent for us. Sure, I sent him messages, but not the usual ones. I was telling him not to do quite as much, can you believe that?

> **The test comes in psychological strength, that extra, undefined toughness.**

Usually the message I send big-time players is: "I'm sick of sitting up here waiting for you to do something."

I worked a lot with Mal Meninga and can tell you he responds to messages, to situations, to everything and anything. Norths, in turn, will look to Jason Taylor, the halfback, and young fullback Matt Seers.

I'm not going to tip either way. Mainly because it is not my job. My job is to coach the Broncos. Do you remember them?

The Broncos made the pre-season final, played in the World Club Championship and finished fourth in the best competition in the world.

They had 10 players involved in the Origin rep games and will have a further half-dozen go away with the Kangaroos.

And you keep asking yourself, what went wrong?

It reminds me of that George Best story.

George Best was a soccer player in England, a trifle controversial but absolutely brilliant.

When he finished he was taking out Miss World.

Together they went to a casino, where George won £60,000. All in one night.

Anyway, he and Miss World returned to their luxury hotel, their pockets, purses and wallets overloaded, and on the way through the foyer George asked the porter if he would be good enough to whip up a bottle of the best French champagne to his suite in about 15 minutes time?

The porter said that wouldn't be a worry, so long as he could ask Mr Best a question once he got there.

No worries.

So the 15 minutes passed and there was a knock on the door.

There's money all over the floor, like confetti. Miss World's there, George is puffing on a great big cigar and the porter's pouring champagne, so carefully because each drop is worth a week's wage.

Finally, he turned and asked the question.

"Mr Best," he said, "what went wrong?"

GIVE ME A HOME
WHERE MONTANAS ROAM

APRIL 1, 1995

God bless America. Sure, I hear the complaints about its loud people and louder traditions but have to admit to sitting on planes coming home and humming *The Star Spangled Banner*.

I could live there, especially around Denver, and would make the move tomorrow if guaranteed regular doses of a match I saw in October last year between the Denver Broncos and the Kansas City Chiefs.

Gridiron can be quite a drawn-out game, it's 4x15-minute quarters stretching to four hours with time-outs and what have you.

This game featured the Broncos' John Elway and the Chiefs' Joe Montana, all-time champion quarterbacks in a game where the quarterback is everything.

They got to the final quarter, only a few points the difference, and there were two unscripted happenings which really should be preserved somewhere and brought out whenever sport is accused of losing its plot.

The first concerned Elway and a cracker pass to a guy who put one foot out of bounds then came back into the field of play before catching the ball. He thought he had a touchdown. Elway thought so too, as did 70,000 fans, all the players and staffs. But not the line judge, and not the head umpire.

You want to talk about pressure.

When these two officials called him out the crowd went crazy. The Denver staff, to a man, headed straight onto the field and towards the two officials. And the players, you had to see the players. The place was just ringing.

Some 20 seconds later Denver scored another touchdown, this time quite legally, and led by four points with just 1 minute 27 seconds on the clock.

> **Montana not only believed he could win that game, everyone in his team and the stadium believed: that's what top players do.**

So to Joe Montana and unscripted happening No. 2.

Denver had to kick off to Kansas City and the stadium hushed because everyone knew there was only one person in the world who could win a game from four points down with 1 minute 27 seconds to go.

Of course I'd heard about Joe Montana, and wondered how much was myth and how much fact. I didn't have to wonder for long. He got the ball 70 metres out, no time-outs left and at 1 minute 20 seconds he drove Kansas to a touch down and triumph.

The guy who took the winning ball had two defenders threatening to kill him, 1 metre from the sideline and 2 metres from glory. He did nothing special. The ball just appeared like magic in the only hole in the packed stadium, somehow blessed by its deliverer.

I don't know what the Chiefs pay Montana, or what San Francisco did before them. I know he's not big or particularly fast or overly strong, but I can tell you I have been in awe of him for precisely 1 minute 27 seconds.

Montana not only believed he could win that game, everyone in his team, the Denver team and the stadium believed: that's what top players do.

Later, we went to the University of Colorado at Boulder where the home team was playing the University of Wyoming. College game, right. Crowd: 60,000.

I counted the players. It's a 44-a-side game. Right. Colorado had 93 players warming up, all taped, rubbed down and in helmets. Wyoming, who had flown in, had 62. It took me a long time, but I counted them.

What I didn't count on was the Colorado mascot, a real-life buffalo which arrives on the back of a truck and drags six large handlers in 300-metre charges down the sidelines at full gallop, the team following.

Just three years ago Colorado lost one of its mascots in the crowd, and they had some fun then, apparently.

Brisbane Broncos have been associated with Denver since we came to be, and I sometimes go to Denver and count: 50 players, 14 coaches.

I thought the best coach I saw . . . I watched him for a couple of days and finally had to ask someone exactly what he did.

"He keeps the time," they said. He what? "We have a meeting and decide what time we'll devote to each discipline at training and when that time's up, this guy blows the whistle."

So I'm looking at him with his feet up on the desk in his big office, all the time being reminded he's very well paid, and I'm thinking: "You lose that whistle fella, and you're out of a job."

I asked somebody what they did to improve their players mentally, and they said they don't do that sort of stuff. Why? Because their players were professionals who were paid lots of money and needed no other motivation, they said.

Which has to be a fallacy. Money is not an issue when it comes to performance.

And they make a lot of videos — videos of the guy making the videos. That's another thing I noticed before leaving for the American Air Force Academy at Colorado Springs.

"The applause soon dies away, the prize left behind, but the character you build up is yours forever."

On the wall at the Academy it says, under the heading The Value of Training: "The duration of an athletic contest is only a few minutes while the training for it may take many weeks of arduous work and continual exercise of self-effort.

"The real value of sport is not the actual game played in the limelight of applause but the hours of dogged determination and self-discipline carried out alone imposed and sequenced by an exacting conscience.

"The applause soon dies away, the prize left behind, but the character you build up is yours forever."

Still, I best liked the one on the wall at Denver Broncos: "Losers assemble in little groups to share their misery and bitch about the coaches and the guys in other little groups. Winners assemble as a team."

Don't tell anyone, but this is how I did the dirty on Brian Smith

June 17, 1995

Brian Smith, I like the way he resigned as coach of St George — it's always nice to get in first.

He's never been a friend of mine but I respect the way he coaches, and the way he never seemed to set out to be popular.

What struck me about his team was that they were always well coached, with good game plans and a desire and ability to stick to them.

That desire and ability, I'm sure, got them into two grand finals but I also thought it was their greatest weakness in the big end-of-season matches.

Perhaps they were too structured to go that one last step. Goodness knows who won more matches overall between St George and us, but I don't have to look up any records to know every one was tough.

One of his statements this week suggested he was disillusioned with the game's direction in this country but, deep down, Brian Smith would be disillusioned by the fact the Dragons have lost six or eight top players to Super League.

That's the thing about coaching, how it's different from being an official, because when you're an official you don't have to worry about results or being accountable.

Brian Smith would realise under the ARL banner it's hard enough to replace one top player but in a split competition it will be impossible to replace six. Having nearly been to the top of the mountain twice, and knowing how hard it was to get there, he would realise it would be many losing seasons before St George climbed back.

Anyway, let's get to the meat of this article. This is a story only my team and a journalist, whom I swore to secrecy, have known.

> **That's the thing about coaching, how it's different from being an official, when you're an official you don't have to worry about results or being accountable.**

Come back to 1993 and the week leading up to the grand final. St George had beaten us in the last competition round at ANZ Stadium, then going into the top three and straight into the grand final whereas, from the bottom, we had to beat Manly, Canberra and Canterbury before getting another crack at them.

The Broncos came into that last week bone-tired, with a lot of injuries. We arrived in Sydney for the traditional grand final breakfast, and back at the airport I ran into a guy who had a lot of friends at St George.

He told me he had the game plan from the 1992 grand final, and also the "tip sheet" Smith had prepared on the Broncos. My eyes lit up and I even grinned. "Would you mind faxing that to me this afternoon," I said.

"Not at all," he said. It duly arrived and I glanced through the game plan but that didn't interest me all that much because the Broncos are rarely concerned about what another team is going to try and do to us.

What caught my eye was the tip sheet. Tip sheets make references player-by-player, comments about strengths and weaknesses. Always looking for the edge, I couldn't believe my luck and rang a friend Bob Bax, who has a great mind for motivation.

I told Bob we needed to spend half an hour together, that I had something important to show him. He couldn't believe his eyes either. Nothing particularly startling, just things like: "Kevin Walters — good hands, quick off the mark: not strong defensively on the left side."

Others summarised by Smith copped it on a quite personal basis, one of our forwards in particular.

What we did, using Smith's terminology, was add little stings to each of the summaries.

Like, "Kevin Walters — along with Allan Langer and brother Kerrod, known as the Ipswich connection; Kevin is the weakness here . . . he's overrated and the other two run around trying to make him look good."

For another we put "lair", another "not tough" . . . "thug".

We had a wonderful time adding these little pieces, and I knew it would be invaluable.

On match eve in the *Weekend Australian*, I said we'd come up with "The Joker". Terry Matterson had a bung shoulder, Glenn Lazarus was crook, Steve Renouf had had just one match back from a busted jaw and Allan Langer was exhausted after Canterbury, so we really did need something special.

My biggest dilemma was when to use it, looking for the right time.

Knowing the players, I knew if we went too early, sure they'd be angry but it would be gone by Sunday. So I held back until a team meeting on game morning. Just produced the pieces of paper and said I'd accidentally come by them and thought every player should sit down and read not just what Brian Smith had to say about them, but more importantly their team-mates.

As they sat there reading, I continued to fuel the fire. "He's not just talking about you, but your team-mates."

The fellow we put in as a "lair" sidled up to me as we were walking out of the room and, laughing, said: "Coach, he's spot on about me." We all laughed together.

> **"He's not just talking about you, but your team-mates."**

Little more was said but just before they went out I reminded them. Of course, we did a tremendous job defensively that afternoon to beat the Dragons for the second time in as many grand finals, and it was generally felt Kevin Walters was outstanding.

What happened after the game: well, things got a bit personal. A few of the players were scathing about Brian Smith and his coaching. Smith couldn't have realised what had happened and I certainly wasn't about to tell anyone.

Alfie Langer topped it off by saying into a microphone: "St George can't play." That didn't help. I told the players but no-one else about it as time passed.

The secret never got out until Mark Hohn joined the Crushers, where he apparently told Wayne Collins, who had left St George to join the same team.

I got a phone call from Chris Johns. Johns said: "Hey coach, Brian Smith's just found out. He's livid. He's trying to find out the mole at St George."

I laughed and laughed. I really enjoyed the witchhunt business, knowing Brian Smith can get a little paranoid. But he's a great competitor and really added something to rugby league in this country. I'll miss him.

When Super League first kicked off, John Ribot rang me and said: "How about Brian Smith?" I had no hesitation in saying he was a good coach and would be a great acquisition.

WAZZABALL
NOT WANTED IN WONDERLAND

AUGUST 6, 1994

In many respects it represented rugby league's Wonderland — but Wazzaball was no fun park.

Brutal, state-of-the-art defence, featuring gang tackling and a game-plan so tight he would get upset if the team scored on the fourth tackle instead of the planned fifth.

He? Warren Ryan, the coach — alongside Jack Gibson, the most influential of the modern era.

His mannerisms, indeed his manner, were different to Big Jack's, but his impact in many areas was just as great.

Warren Ryan brought science to coaching. Too few people know he represented Australia at the 1962 Commonwealth Games in Perth and realised the weights which assisted him in shotput could be just as helpful to others in our game.

They called him a "defensive coach", which was a fallacy. Whenever anyone in any walk of life is particularly talented in one area, the knockers want to make out he or she is bad in another.

No-one could have had the success Warren Ryan has without being great both sides of the ruck.

To me, game-plans came with him. There are so many stories, the way he made his teams so committed to the game-plan — neat game-plans, too. In six years his teams featured in five grand finals.

Players had to take the ball to a certain position on the field and do nothing else until they arrived there. He came up with this line theory, based on the width of the field.

Whether defending or on the attack, his sides worked to percentage points — 10 per cent being near the sideline, 50 per cent mid-field . . . say the ball was at 30 per cent, that meant only so many players, perhaps three, were required to defend on the short side no matter how many attackers were there.

I remember when Steve Mortimer, one of Ryan's captains at Canterbury, made the point that Warren would become quite agitated if they scored on the fourth tackle instead of the fifth or on the right-hand side of the field instead of the planned left.

> **No-one could have had the success Warren Ryan has without being great both sides of the ruck.**

Not wanting to sound negative in any way, but when I came into Winfield Cup coaching I had a big decision to make: I either had to become very game-plan oriented, that is Wazzaball, a la Warren Ryan and, subsequently, Phil Gould, or I had to form an attack to blow these great defences away.

For 12 months I studied Canterbury's play.

History shows which way I went, and that it obviously worked, but it did take time, through Canberra in '87 and two or three years at the Broncos.

What we had to learn to master was the constant pressure Ryan's team would put us under, all the time remembering Ryan's team never beat itself.

His coaching record against me was very much in his favour, but I never thought about it in a negative way, and when we did start to win against Balmain, when we mastered it, I felt we had somehow grown up as a team.

Finally, our players totally understood the continued pressure, the waves of them coming at us, so relentless and forever prepared to feed off our mistakes.

During our learning period, Balmain enjoyed a 6–0 record against us . . . then, one day in Brisbane, we broke free — got it right.

I don't know Warren Ryan all that well, but he certainly has plenty of confrontation about him.

The thing about him that stands out to me is the way he never wavered from his beliefs. Just the other day I read somewhere that one of his former players has said Warren never had any trouble handling men. Players can be such prima donnas at times, unable to accept criticism, and I read into that remark what I had suspected — thin-skinned players were never going to cut it with Warren Ryan.

He can be quite harsh, but at the end of the day he got results and I think, no, I know, that's what a coach is paid for.

He was always a little paranoid about his set plays and others using them, but I wonder whether we, that is modern coaches, changed the game all that much. It's not like we've invented the wheel or anything important.

When NSW scored that try off the set play involving Bradley Clyde, I remember Warren blowing up.

Bob Lindner was playing under Warren at Wests and the following night, when Bob turned up at training, Warren very quickly informed him that it was his move and that Phil Gould, the Blues coach, had pinched it and as far as he was concerned it was Warren Ryan six, NSW six.

One of the things Warren is strong on, and I don't disagree, is that there's simply not enough good players to go around.

No matter what anyone says there are some players at some clubs this moment getting top dollars and they are not top first graders.

I think this, as much as anything else, led to his exit at Western Suburbs.

I'm not trying to put them down, but if you're going to coach, unless you have the job at

> **"What this game needs is old heads on young bodies."**
> KELVIN GILES

one of the top clubs, it's only ever a matter of time. They're going to point the bone at you, just like they did to him.

It's a strange old game. In other sports, competitors get old. Runners get old, swimmers. But in rugby league, they can hide, go forever. Nobody ever loses form. The media tell the player he's doing fine, the fans cheer, and it's just the silly old coach who says he's hopeless.

Kelvin Giles, at our place, got it right when he said what this game needs is old heads on young bodies.

The thing I'm saying is that there was less wrong with Warren Ryan's head than there was with the bodies down at Campbelltown. They wanted Wonderland, not Wazzaball. They simply didn't understand.

STRADDLING A FINE LINE BETWEEN EGOMANIA AND EXCELLENCE

JULY 29, 1995

Many guys, courtesy of that squeaky old rumour mill, will have the job of replacing Tim Sheens as Canberra Raiders coach long before anyone actually does.

Because of the work they've done and Tim Sheens' involvement, the Raiders are in an ideal situation, so powerful.

They can approach any coach in the world and get him for 1997.

Sure, Tim's leaving, but the team is not and the organisation is not.

If I can give them a little advice, I strongly suggest not getting a coach with an inflated ego.

I'm not sure how you measure ego but the Raiders need a gadget able to ensure the new guy's ego sits easily with continued development, rather than someone intimidated by what Tim's done or what the players have done.

They want a coach with the attitude: "I just want to be part of the continued success — not the centrepiece."

Get someone wanting to be the centrepiece, and down comes the club just like London Bridge.

Someone may come in wanting to stamp his authority and his ways and his methods, but no-one is going to do a much better job than has been done.

One of the more silly moves would be to appoint a coach with no experience, straight out of the playing ranks, because the players would be coaching the coach.

If I were Canberra, the chairman or chief executive, I'd just get the best coach in the world no matter the obstacles placed between me and him.

Any other strategy and it's London Bridge time.

Look at Parramatta. A decade ago precisely, they were about to win their fourth premiership in five years, Jack Gibson having taken them to three in a row.

Balmain, what about Balmain? Grand finalists in 1988 and '89, more than unlucky not to have won one of them, and then what? Warren Ryan leaves, that's what, and down it comes.

There's this fine line, and often you wonder on which side of it you're standing? You think the success is going to hang around through a decade, maybe forever, but mostly you're wrong.

Coaches leave, players begin leaving, there are poor coaching appointments, poor recruitment . . . it all adds up.

Conversely, look at the Cowboys and how they've just about assured themselves of success by signing Tim Sheens.

Already the Cowboys have the crowds and a lot of good things there. Now they've capped things with a coach whose appointment will attract fine players who might have otherwise sidestepped the joint.

> **You think the success is going to hang around through a decade, maybe forever, but mostly you're wrong.**

I'm not trying to put up the stocks of coaches by saying everything revolves around us, because it doesn't.

What makes one club successful and another spending the same money and putting in the same hours unsuccessful is, first up, the chairman or chief executive or a combination or both.

Strong people in the front office attract other strong people, whether it be in sport or business — not that there is any difference these days.

That sounds an airy-fairy sort of line, but it's a fact of life.

People who stand for something and are respected just don't attract the fools, the floaters of life, and that filters down to all the staff, including the coach.

The right coach is attracted by the right head man and then builds a team around him of the right players: players attracted by his strength and he by their's.

Some organisations, like Canberra, stand the test of time. The Raiders have missed the playoffs only once since 1987. Australian football league club Hawthorn have played in the last 13 semi-final series.

Hawthorn's had different coaches, Canberra basically the one, but the similarity is that both have been led by strong men with good organisations behind them.

> **"Success is not forever — and failure isn't fatal."**
> DON SHULA

When talk turns to successful football clubs it's not complete, there's no fullstop, until mention of the Miami Dolphins.

With win No. 325, the Dolphins' Don Shula has just become the most successful coach in National Football League history.

Shula says of leadership: "The biggest problem with most leaders of today is they don't stand for anything.

"Convictions provide that direction. If you don't stand for something, you fall for everything."

However inadvertently, Don Shula has helped me a lot this week. His favourite saying is: "Success is not forever — and failure isn't fatal."

He says once you accept that, there is the capacity to rebound.

COACHES INTEGRAL, BUT NOT WINNERS

JUNE 11, 1994

When friends ring to tell me they have just been appointed coach, I always say: "Commiserations."

It's a bit like that: you chase the job, and really want it — but the job has a lot of pitfalls.

In two or three years they will have fallen out with everyone. Their wives and the fans, the committee, of course, and all they'll have left is, well, not much.

There's not much difference between the general manager of a company, an army officer or a coach. It is important they have a pretty strong will, know where they want to be going, they're committed and not easily distracted.

Pope John Paul II said: "See everything, overlook a great deal — and prove a little." I like that.

There is so much to see and do and while you have to see it all, you can never do it all.

Many coaches, they see the big picture but never manage to narrow it down to improve small areas before moving on.

As for being strong-willed, hey, the fans and the family, sometimes the players, they'll all be telling you what should be done. Start listening to fans, though, and it won't be long before you're over there sitting with them.

That's a key part, standing by decisions, being confident that you're going to make enough good ones. Having a plan.

The biggest mistake a coach can make is to not be himself, if he

can be manipulated. You can have love affairs with pla
that's OK — but remain strong enough to know
using you up.

I say, look, if they're going to sack you, when you walk out
door do it with no regrets, leave with pride and self-esteem.
Listen to others and, don't worry, they're going to sack you
anyway.

No-one can coach without discipline but make too many rules
and there are just more to break. Don't complicate matters, just
give the players a framework not too fancy to work within.

And motivation. The unmotivated cannot be motivated. When
I first coached and saw a player with talent but bad attitude at
another club, a player going nowhere, I'd go for him. It was
always his old coach's fault and I could turn him around. But I
was wrong. It wasn't the coach, it was the player and it just
reminded me that wherever you go, you have to take yourself.

Coaches don't win, players win, and a coach is not as smart as
people say when their team wins nor as stupid as they say when
they lose.

At day's end the trick is to improve the player, to have him
playing at, or close to his ability.

In the Winfield Cup, the stark
reality is there are 15 losing
coaches every year and from
1996 the odds can only get
worse. They can't all fail — and
they don't.

> **"See everything,
> overlook a
> great deal — and
> prove a little."**
> POPE JOHN PAUL II

There are two types: the coach that builds and the one out
there looking for a quick fix. The quick-fix coach comes in, upsets
everyone and everything, gets some results, but within two or
three years his organisation is in tatters.

Ring some bells?

I love the coach who says: "I coached good but the boys, the
bloody boys, didn't they play bad?"

Bear Bryant, the great American coach, wanted the respect of
his players if not their love, and I can say when things have been
bad my players have always supported me.

As Bear Bryant said: "If anything goes bad — I did it. If anything goes good — good, we did it. If anything goes really, really good — congratulations fellas, you did it."

wayne
B E N N E T T

ON FOOTBALL POLITICS

In the changerooms,
rugby league is still sport. It's the same on
the field. But not in the real world, out there
it's simply, clinically business.

DREAM LIVES
AS DARKNESS DESCENDS

FEBRUARY 27, 1996

It is darker than night.

Sitting next to me on the train is a fan, not one that blows cool air but a footy fan. Behind us is a player, and in front a club executive. It's the same all round — fans and coaches and players and executives and darkness.

I tell you this because you can't see either, and the reason you can't see is because we're in a tunnel and the lights are out.

The two guys driving the train answer to the names of Rupert Murdoch and Ken Cowley, and we know when they finally take us out of this tunnel only two things can happen: we're either going to see lots of glorious daylight, or we're going to have one almighty crash.

At times it's hard to know what's rattling more, the train or some of the passengers.

A couple of questions keep flashing through the mind. Why, for starters, are these players still sitting there, showing such solidarity, when they could have easily jumped to the ARL's cruise liner? And, two, why has Rupert Murdoch, through his staff here in Australia, shown such great strength and commitment towards Super League?

Sure, in the beginning — April Fool's Day, 1995 — there's no doubting money had a tremendous influence on everything and almost everyone and still the cynics speak about us doing it for the money every time we stand up and say something positive about Super League.

Laurie Daley stands up and says he doesn't want a bar of the ARL competition. Is that simply because of the money? Daley, and the other champion players. You and I both know that they could have earned as much if not more money had they gone the other way. No, this whole affair runs much deeper than dollars. It's about an alternative, about things as simple as being heard and being respected . . . about starting afresh.

This might well surprise a lot of people, but there are as many people in Super League who love the game as there are on the other side.

Global exposure is important. Why? Simply because we believe it's a great game. In the past, there has been no vision, no genuine attempts to expand beyond this country.

The Broncos' Chris Johns says how he wants to be part of the best and not be embarrassed by the fact it is restricted to two states of Australia. Chris sees the big picture, wanting people in America and Europe to see the game he plays.

We go to America and want to see a gridiron game. Chris Johns, for one, wants Americans getting off the plane and asking where the closest game of footy is. He talks five years ahead and, indeed, Super League is not about today, it's about tomorrow — today is already too late. Walt Disney always dreamt about tomorrow. That's part of the reason Walt Disney was great.

Then I look at Rupert Murdoch, and I wonder some more. Already it has cost he and Ken Cowley lots of heartache and personal criticism. This guy, obviously, knows a bit about business, and he understands we've been underselling our game for 100 years.

In football, we have all suffered concussion, been knocked out . . . but some of us still haven't had enough headaches to give up.

Rupert Murdoch, more than most, understands all things are difficult before they are easy.

I know this fella in America, he plays out of left field. Goes to Country Fairs, see . . . walks in under the arches and heads straight to the flea section.

Forget the clowns, the elephants and the merry-go-rounds, this fella is always headed towards the fleas.

> **"If you're skating on thin ice, you may as well tap dance."**
> BRYCE COURTENAY

For ages he just stood there looking at them jumping up and down in glass canisters. The fleas don't jump out, ever, even though the canisters have no lids.

Finally, being an inquisitive fella, he seeks out the flea trainer.

Flea trainer says: "It's all in the way you start with them."

Huh?

"Well, you put 'em in the jar, whack a plastic lid on it and the new fleas begin jumping up and down, bashing their little flea-brains on the top. After enough headache experiences, they stop jumping quite so high and settle in their comfort zone.

"It's then that I'm in a position to take off the lid and they'll be contained in that jar forever more, not by a lid but by a mindset that says so high and no more."

In football, we have all suffered concussion, been knocked out . . . but some of us still haven't had enough headaches to give up.

Some of us still want to jump . . . higher than high.

As Bryce Courtenay wrote: "If you're skating on thin ice, you may as well tap dance."

No character,
NO INTEGRITY — NOTHING

MAY 27, 1995

If the rumour mill has speeds, the rugby league one is at full throttle right now and has been since those Canterbury players jumped the line back to the Australian Rugby League.

The calls began arriving at the Broncos on Tuesday: "You're next," they all said, "next on the hit list."

But only one of our players, Julian O'Neill, was approached, inspired by Bob Fulton but through a third party.

Fulton, of course, has acted on behalf of the ARL with our players before. When they signed with the Super League on the Monday, Fulton, James Packer and John Quayle hit Brisbane on the Wednesday for talks with seven of our guys.

The following day we had a meeting of our own, getting Super League chief executive John Ribot on a phone hook-up to clarify a few things which were concerning the players, questions planted by the ARL posse.

Yes, there would definitely be a Super League. No, it was not all riding on the back of a $2 shelf company. Things like that.

The money offered our players by the ARL was always more than Super League, and, during the phone hook-up, I had a solicitor there to help the players — we wanted to railroad nobody.

But once we had talked to John we were quite satisfied and I remember the solicitor saying afterwards: "You really have a group of men here with a great deal of character."

With everything that has happened in this battle those few words have been the most significant aspect to me. As I often say to them: If we fail as footballers, hey, we can handle that: but if we show no character, no integrity, this has all been a waste of time.

Since April 1, the Broncos have shown a tremendous amount of character in every sense. The thing that Super League did — and this is irrelevant to Jarrod McCracken, Allan Langer and Ricky Stuart — but why I will feel indebted to it for the rest of my life is it recognised the John Plaths, Peter Ryans, Andrew Gees and Alan Canns of this footballing world.

> **If we fail as footballers, hey, we can handle that: but if we show no character, no integrity, this has all been a waste of time.**

Under the previous restrictions of the salary cap, these were the guys who most suffered. We knew they were not going anywhere this week. It's the so-called cream the ARL chases and I just rang the players to let them know what to expect.

It's funny, but when I rang Allan Langer I said: "Alf, you might get a phone call — but you won't!"

The last time they spoke to the Broncos, Alfie didn't get a call and if you know him you know why. When Allan Langer makes a decision, that's it. It's all over.

Bob Fulton, his Australian coach, knows that only too well. If he did get the call, he would be nice, mumble into his blond beard for a while then say sorry and hang up.

I told the others not to encourage them by talking for too long . . . that the ARL agents were used-car salesmen at the moment, desperate to do a deal. We have already done a deal, I said, it's over. They said: "That's fine, coach."

You're always worried, that's why you call, but they have never failed me, the players, and all of them are accustomed to being offered more money to leave.

O'Neill made the best point. He said: "Gee, it would be nice to pay off my house . . . but the only problem is I couldn't live in it, couldn't live with myself."

I know what he means because I once broke a contract and feel bad about it to this day.

It was at Canberra. I had a four-year deal and was halfway through the first year when the Broncos were born. My whole life was Queensland, but when they came to me I said no.

In the end, after many talks, they sold me the car, and the last thing we spoke about was money. I'd taken the job, committed, before it came to cash, I said: "I don't want a cent less than I'm getting at Canberra, and not a cent more."

Still, I felt lousy and do whenever I think of Canberra and the way I left. When I ring players today I'm not acting on behalf of Super League but just trying to keep a great club great, together.

They hear about the $780,000 a season for McCracken and think, that's all right. It's like Malcolm Reilly, the Newcastle coach. The ARL gave him $300,000, and guys like Peter Louis at Norths, they get nothing. But what they do is get on with their lives.

I saw McCracken on the television last night and I don't think he realises the pressure he has put himself under.

As young men, they just don't realise. Through the court cases, the interviews — it's OK saying we'll back you, and we'll do this, but what is this "we" business, Kemosabe?

When it's all over I'm sure those four Bulldogs will look

> **Let's all go our own way, see what happens in two or three years. I certainly have no fears. None.**

back and wish they had done it differently. Those solicitors telling both sides they can win, right, that's why there are so many solicitors out there.

They all have a point of view but in the end the solicitor walks away and no-one has questioned his character or integrity. He has no scars.

I felt for Bulldogs coach Chris Anderson and agree with what he said in the paper, how his club had made a decision, so why couldn't they be left alone?

The ARL has taken away from our players the right to

represent, and if they are right, if Super League is going to fall over, why worry? Why pester, interfere?

As Chris Anderson said, we want no part of the ARL concept — we have our own.

Let's all go our own way, see what happens in two or three years. I certainly have no fears. None.

COMMITTEES SHOULD
STRIVE FOR THE COMMON GOOD

MAY 13, 1995

This is for all you old farts. I've been amazed and justly intrigued to read this week about the reinstatement in England of Will Carling, then poor Arthur Tunstall fell on his sword, again.

And it made me think about the committee, which all of us in sport have experienced, made me realise if Moses had been on a committee the Israelites would still be in Egypt.

Rugby has had more than its share of problems with committees and as a friend said recently when talk turned to paying rugby union players: "What do you mean, are they going to pay tax now?"

I heard John O'Shea, a Welshman who has lived in Australia for 20-odd years, and a wonderful speaker, referring to the Welsh rugby committee back 20 or 30 years ago.

They had 125 on the committee and no room big enough to fit in that many chairs so they all sat on top of one another at meetings.

Beaten by Western Samoa for the first time ever, a committeeman, upon getting off the floor, said: "Mr Chairman, this has been a terrible day for Welsh rugby — but it could have been worse: at least it was only the West, not the whole of Samoa that beat us."

The great majority of committee guys have never made a decision in their lives. Never had any authority, anywhere, and the wife's always told them what to do. But I always find out more about their thoughts and aspirations after a meeting because some never talk at the meeting.

After a few drinks, they are quick to tell all and sundry exactly what they said, how they strenuously challenged so and so and the monumental changes they're going to implement.

I remember Big Sammy Backo just after he retired. He had been on the committee of a hotel and making a little bit of a pest of himself, so they started having meetings without him.

Sam, being a prop, wasn't that silly and soon realised his considerable chair was empty in the committee room when it should not have been. Not to be outdone, Sam apologised, saying that he'd missed a couple of the meetings. He said to the boss: "In future I will set the time, the date and the agenda." So that's what he did.

> **A lot of committees are like the Senate: ageless old men mumbling at each other.**

Former soccer manager Tommy Docherty summed it up when he said the best committee is the committee of three — two are dead, and one's dying.

A lot of committees are like the Senate: ageless old men mumbling at each other. One of the good ones belongs to Jack Gibson. After they got rid of the 42-man NSWRL committee, Jack reckoned that the tucker bill alone would have saved them a fortune.

Have you ever noticed the committeeman after a loss, how he comes down talking to the players and blames the coach?

If he's talking to the coach, he blames the players. Then, if he's talking to both the coach and the players, he blames the referee.

When they win, though, it's always how smart they were getting such a fine team of players and coaches together instead of, in the losing situation: "Who is responsible for buying this team?"

The real kiss of death in our business is when they have a vote of confidence in you.

Here at the Broncos I have told the committee you can come out and say anything you want, do anything you want, just never have a vote of confidence in me — that's when I know I'm finished.

The purpose of a committee and board is surely to strive for the common good of the people and the sport they are representing, right. They're not there for their own glorification and trips, and the feeling of power should not be the driving force for any person.

Ghandi once said there are two kinds of people — those who do the work and those who take the credit. Be in the first group, there's less competition.

Behind every sacked coach, there's a chairman.

One thing that really fascinates me about the Super League debate is how the club committees haven't been able to dictate the agenda.

But when I think more deeply, I realise it's because of the cynical things I've mentioned here — they've come back to haunt them.

I remember saying to John Ribot before he'd go out for one of those silly chief executive meetings, why?

He'd tell me how they'd voted 16–0 for a change in the game, or direction, whatever, then they'd get rolled by the board.

I just got angry, telling John I couldn't be part of that. If the clubs vote unanimously, how can they lose? I said, "you're wasting your time going."

This is our game.

Maurice Lindsay made a good point recently, and I suppose before telling you that, we have never had a vote at the Broncos on anything. "I don't like votes," said Lindsay, "because whenever there's a vote there's a loser."

I think, in our business, the ideal committee is made up of proven businessmen, maybe one or two of them, certainly a legal person, a chairperson, an accountant, and one or two people from the sport with background. The smaller the better.

But I'm afraid most are made up of nodders, some sleeping nodders some just plain old nodders. I've never tried to win friends on a committee because you can never please them all, so I don't bother trying.

Again reverting to Jack Gibson: "The hardest part about being in a winning side is to first train the committee."

Top referees,
like players, don't mature overnight

April 29, 1995

This is about Super League, referees and experience.

The most immediate effect Super League is having on the competition are the defections, or sackings, of referees joining the so-called rebel competition.

I have serious reservations about the league's sacking decision, and not just because the referees have been victimised whereas the players have not — for now. There's also the impact the decision will have on the Winfield Cup.

Go back to the 1994 grand final and referee Greg McCallum's leaving Australia virtually at fulltime for an appointment in England.

During the off-season I went to England and some guy strutted up asking what I was doing there?

"Just making sure Greg McCallum arrived safely and likes the place enough to stay for a very long time," I said.

Four new teams this year and McCallum's departure meant we needed three new referees. Now another four referees, including three of the game's most experienced, have shot off to Super League. This means seven of the 10 current first grade referees were in a different grade last year.

One of the most difficult coaching assignments is replacing players. From vast experience I know the Broncos can lose three or four players and still be competitive.

Once we begin looking at more than four the new ones are nowhere near as effective, however.

It's not because they don't try hard or they're not conscientious — it's just that they lack experience and, in some cases, mightn't even have the talent.

Talent? They have the talent to play rugby league, but not enough of it to reach the high standard required.

Why in sport do people always talk about experience? I have a theory on this: it's because it's important, that's why.

Like with the old manager. He's retiring. The young guy taking over walks in, says: "Pop, one of your great strengths as a manager was that you made lots of great decisions."

"I made them by experience," says the old man.

"Hope I can do as good," says the kid.

Old guy says: "You get the experience by the bad decisions." And then he walks away.

The inexperienced referee has everybody judging his decisions.

The experienced referee makes bad decisions too, just like the top players make mistakes. The difference is the players will accept the odd mistake from the top ref — but not from the new boy.

I saw an interesting game recently where one of the younger referees was asked to control one of the more experienced teams, and its players worked continually to intimidate him.

One opposition score produced possibly the worst exhibition I've seen in years.

The great majority of the experienced team's senior players, very aggressive and forceful, swooped on this inexperienced referee like buzzards.

Like all of us the referee, when alone, is dictated to by self-talk.

If he's making bad decisions he's not like a player who can get support from team-mates.

Why in sport do people always talk about experience? Because it's important, that's why.

This guy's self-talk can be very negative and destructive, leading to a lack of concentration and, in some cases, panic.

Then you've got the crowd and its behaviour. One thing about crowds; they always hate to see their teams being beaten but become absolutely furious at a perceived lack of experience from the guy with the whistle.

So the ref's self-talk is negative, the crowd's out of control — so boisterous. Suddenly, there's a bad decision and the players begin taking things into their own hands.

Once one team realises the other is refereeing the game, they want to as well.

I believe referees will become a much greater discussion point between players and coaches before games from now on.

You're not supposed to find out who is in control until match day but usually the information is around by the Tuesday.

I've never phoned anyone to find out the referee for a Broncos match but I will now. The situation is that you don't find seven new referees of first grade standard in a few months, no way.

Players either. You bring them along gradually. One of the real problems with inexperienced players is over-exposing them. Sometimes, if you give them too much too soon, it takes them a while to come back. Other times, sadly, they never come back.

If I were a young, inexperienced ref right now I wouldn't be listening to any radios or reading the newspapers. Just last week, in the Illawarra–Crushers match the ref sent one player off, and he was later exonerated. He missed another two. They were put on report by the respective clubs, found guilty and suspended. At one stage, the team which finished one short led 18–2. Perhaps the same thing could have happened with an experienced referee, but no-one's interested.

My goal for the rest of this year is to get the Broncos into the match-of-the-day every week. That way we've a chance of getting one of the top three referees. When we're out in the backwoods playing, with no TV cameras and not much else . . . they're certainly going to be long days at the office.

WARNING:
HUNGER AND HURRICANES

MAY 14, 1994

When did the end begin? This isn't easy to know. There's never been an announcement when a dynasty dies, no voice of doom proclaiming that you are slipping . . . down from the mountaintop, down to where the also-rans live . . .

I'm sitting here reading the April 18 edition of the American publication *Sports Illustrated*, the story headed "Hurricane Warning" and to do with the University of Miami Hurricanes, college football's premier team.

It has nothing to do with the Broncos, but I'm reading it anyway.

I look to America to study if not learn a lot of things because everything's privately owned in America and when things are privately owned there is the right marketing, the right facilities whatever.

The sole reason is the individuals who own the franchise drive it.

We're privately owned, the Broncos, and therefore unique in the Winfield Cup.

I've worked under the other system, too, and from a coaching point of view felt a lot more pressure at the Broncos.

There's nothing wrong with pressure, and I'm not complaining — certainly I'm in favour of clubs going into private ownership.

In the other situation the first or second thing you hear about a club is how its leagues club is going because survival is dependent on dollars from leagues clubs.

Privately-owned clubs, though, they're dependent on their owners — it's a big difference.

The Broncos are driven by the directors' desire not to take losses and we all realise if we don't work a little harder, if we're a bit skirmish about the hard decisions, then we'll start to make the club vulnerable.

I worked for the government for 20-odd years and feel that for a lot of other clubs it's like working for the government because they're virtually assured of an income and assured of their losses being picked up by the leagues clubs.

> **In a private situation, if you don't perform you don't have a job, don't get paid.**

In a private situation, if you don't perform you don't have a job, don't get paid.

Crusaders — but every rugby league club in England is now privately owned.

The benefits are everybody's thinking commercially because if the losses do occur it's the owners' homes and families who suffer.

It's more personal.

If, say, the coach doesn't do the job properly we all pay the price — sponsorship's down, crowd figures are down.

I probably felt the pressure more in the early years at the Broncos, knowing a bad season now wouldn't hurt too much but a couple back-to-back would.

I was a great admirer of that magnificent football team of the late '70s early '80s Parramatta, and still remember marvelling at their crowd figures and corporate sponsorship.

But in the '90s the crowds and sponsorship at Parramatta are not what they were.

Cycles? Yeah, I believe in them a bit. The part with it is to be never down at the bottom. You go through tremendous years and come off it a little bit perhaps but the trick is to still be competitive and stay within reach for the climb back.

John Quayle, the NSWRL general manager, last year made a song and dance about the Broncos making money by selling

20 per cent of the company to Northern Rivers Holdings, but I figure if you're going to take a risk in life you deserve a dividend.

Privatisation, of course, is fraught with danger. We're all familiar with the Sydney Swans, and Gold Coast who were privately owned when they entered the Winfield Cup only to see their three owners sell out.

West Coast Eagles started out in AFL privately owned and the Broncos have certainly had their losses, too.

We are owned and run by four people — the chairman Paul Morgan, Gary Balkin, Steve Williams and Barry Maranta, and about once a month I meet with these directors.

A few years ago when we were out of form and a Brisbane television station was conducting a poll on whether or not I should be sacked, unbeknown to me on the day the poll results were to be released the directors had a meeting and decided to renew my contract.

I never signed it but can't help thinking about the local politician . . . they had a phone poll asking whether or not this guy should remain mayor of a country town and after a bit of investigating found he had used his mobile phone 400 times to register the "yes" vote.

In our first year we played South Sydney on a Friday night and performed terribly — worst ever. Queensland had just won the State of Origin, which I was coaching, too, and we (the Broncos) were all terribly embarrassed the following Friday night.

> **I figure if you're going to take a risk in life you deserve a dividend.**

Anyway, we got home and I got the message from chief executive John Ribot that the directors wanted to see me.

I was pretty pumped up, not wanting to go through this routine and they were quite challenging.

But they forgot I'd played with two of them — Paul Morgan and Steve Williams — and I reminded them subtly of a couple of their more-than-ordinary performances as players, explaining the Broncos were no different.

The bottom line is we've never had another of those meetings.

Reading this *SI* article and nearing the end, I see Miami coach Dennis Erickson says: "I'm hungrier right now than I've ever been in my life. People better get ready to play us because we're going to come after their ass."

Still, as I said before, it has nothing to do with the Broncos.

Shared visions
made decision right

April 8, 1995

The important thing about life is making *the* decision, about courage and character.

Sure I dream and have often considered the ideal world in rugby league but never dared to think anyone had the courage to chase it. Perhaps I underrated the Murdoch organisation and its Australian chief Ken Cowley.

Cowley is 60 years of age and could easily have sat on his hands content with running such a successful business but he didn't.

The perspective to me, look, I know Rupert Murdoch and Ken Cowley are businesspeople and at day's end they've got to make a dollar.

But I know John Ribot, too, and he has never done anything for money.

I never dreamt that Rupert Murdoch and Ken Cowley, that type of person, would come into this game and share the same visions as myself.

One of the great fallacies being spread by the ARL, is that football is not a business. They're still making out it's a sport. They must not see the player walking in with his accountant, his manager and solicitor, another digit in the entertainment business.

What I try to do as a coach is, when all the deals are done, I try to bring sport into it. In the changerooms, rugby league is still sport. It's the same on the field. But not in the real world, out there it's simply, clinically business.

The Broncos were in Auckland for the first round of the competition when John Ribot came to me explaining: "I've got something pretty important to tell you." I said: "It's not that bloody Super League again, is it?" He said: "Yes."

"You guys must be crazy." To which Ribot said: "No, we're going to get it right this time." We went for a jog together and I loved the words I heard.

Normally I run away from John Ribot when we jog but that time in Auckland I raced to keep by his side.

John Ribot, I know, has had messages on his table for the past month to ring James Packer. But he never rang. Everyone's been wanting to do a deal with him, wanting him to drop off Super League, but he won't listen.

Around Auckland Harbour he told me what News Corp wanted to do, about the mentality of the challenge, the energy, the sacrifices and the dollar.

How Super League was going to do things for the game that people had only ever dreamed of.

The ARL have never done what Rupert Murdoch intends to do, and Kerry Packer could never do it either. England, in regards rugby league, had been dying until given a lifeline by News this week and, as I was driving home today, I could not help but think Allan Langer, Ricky Stuart, Laurie Daley and Steve Renouf will soon be recognised around the world instead of just Australia.

In 10 years' time the game will be played at the highest level in Japan, America, Africa and people will say, hey, that's Alfie Langer like they say that's Joe Montana. Those satellites are amazing things.

As a kid growing up, you made a decision on whether you are going to be greedy or do things for the right reason.

We just kept jogging, and even when we finished I wouldn't leave John alone. He told me that he was going to look after me as a coach, but I said: "Just tell me what's in it for the players." Some are now earning $4 million, and that's great. If a guy can earn $4 million and the club can make a profit, so be it.

I was poor, sure I've been poor. As a kid growing up, you made a decision on whether you are going to be greedy or do things for the right reason.

I know John Ribot made the same decision as I and it wouldn't matter what they offered him, he's going to do the right thing.

Australian coach Bob Fulton rang Glenn Lazarus on Tuesday wanting to talk and Big Lazo said: "I've signed with Super League."

Fulton told him that he could get out of it if he wanted to, that he had a solicitor sitting next to him and they could challenge the contract because it was signed under duress.

> **Some of the behaviour by both sides I don't necessarily agree with, but that's life.**

"To be honest," said Lazo, "I wasn't under too much duress — I left the room with the biggest cheque I've seen in my life and felt like dancing on the tables."

I'm outspoken on my Super League views because I believe it's right, I know it's right. Some of the behaviour by both sides I don't necessarily agree with, but that's life. What is unacceptable is that there's a guy called Ruben Wiki who can't play football at the moment because he signed two contracts.

Where's the sense in that? The Australian coach is ringing players and inducing them to break contracts. How can that happen?

The general manager of the league, John Quayle, is supposed to be the number one statesman of the game. The other day he came to Brisbane and, after meeting with a few of my players, told the press he had made no financial offers to them. John Quayle, along with Bob Fulton and James Packer offered each of those players $300,000 cash presents to be paid within seven days of them signing with the league.

So why say that? I'm not going to coach Queensland in the Origin Series if the League bars the best players, but I'm optimistic, someone somewhere will stand up and be counted.

Whether or not Bob Fulton and John Quayle want to admit it, the League raced around signing Australian and NSW players but totally forgot about Queensland and Origin.

The League had always operated as a network, and I know they think they are as right as I think they are wrong. They have forgotten how to let the truth surface. That's not being corny, and I know the ARL believe in what they are doing. It's just that they're wrong.

I wasn't at all impressed when I first met Ken Cowley.

You know, he really wasn't up to date with the game and some of the things he was saying about the players and their futures didn't make a lot of sense.

But that was a fair while ago when News was still attempting to go through the front door of Phillip Street with a good concept but seemingly lacking in courage.

I probably thought Cowley and his mob were wimps. I said: "John (Ribot), you're kidding yourself hanging around with these guys." But I've changed my mind.

They were knocked down flat, and they got going again and now I know they have something going for them.

I have spoken to Ken Cowley on a couple of occasions of late and he really has his eyes on it now, so focused, and there's a kindness and sincerity about him that makes you want to work for him.

You just feel that he's telling no lies, that he can make a decision without having to go back and talk to the committee.

> **"Even if you are on the right track, you'll get run over if you just sit there."**

Look at what happened to Illawarra coach Graham Murray this week. His board up and sacked him. Peter Mulholland rang me from Perth about the same time and said: "I think I'm gone too." The coaches, we've been keeping each other going all week. In a way I was pleased Illawarra sacked Graham Murray. Not for him, I was sorry for him, but the decision reinforced what I think is wrong with the game and the people running it.

Who are Illawarra to sack Graham Murray? That's the board that let John Simon go, the board that won't find another halfback like him for more than a decade. They went to Phillip Street for help but were told there was no money. But there was some money last Saturday morning don't worry, but it was too late for Illawarra.

The League actually told one club chairman that his outfit would not be expelled from the competition so long as he went home and put his coach's head on a block.

Now each club, through Super League, has $4 million to spend on players and the great thing about it as far as I'm concerned is that I guess you could call them unfashionable players like John Plath, Peter Ryan, Brett Galea, Alan Cann and Andrew Gee . . . they haven't played a lot of Test matches, and their wages have been virtually nothing — now they are getting some real money out of the game and they're the height of fashion.

I'm still waiting for the ARL to ring up if not look after players like Plath, Ryan, Galea, Cann and Gee.

One of my senior players during the week said: "Coach, I've got to look after myself." I can understand that, but I've got to look after the team.

It's been a tough old week, a lot of pain, but I'm happy because I just know we're on the right track.

The best fun has been reading the cliches on the desk calendar.

One day this week, it said: "Even if you are on the right track, you'll get run over if you just sit there." The next one said: "Don't agonise, organise." And, finally, today it said: "Half the failures in life arise from pulling in one's horse, just as he is leaping."

I like that.

wayne BENNETT

ON ROGUES AND ROLE MODELS

---

*For the great majority
of us . . . the search is for role models, for
appealing qualities and characteristics.*

ROLE MODEL RECIPE IS NO SECRET: INGREDIENTS COME FROM WITHIN

MAY 6, 1995

For the great majority of us, particularly in our adolescent years, the search is for role models, for appealing qualities and characteristics.

We're all looking for a direction in life, to be better — the smart ones are anyway.

One of the misconceptions about role models is that they have to be football stars, rock singers or politicians, anyone at all with a high profile.

Most of my role models were never superstars at anything, just good people.

There's a responsibility that goes with all of us: it has to do with the way people are always looking at you, watching your every move. And they don't tell you they're looking, they just do it.

At dinner the other night I was thinking about this column, sitting there with my two daughters. The 17-year-old said her parents were her role models: and it just reminded me that she's been watching her mum and dad for a long time.

Obviously, by her comments, she has been developing her personality on our actions and behaviour.

My 13-year-old daughter said: "What are role models. Dad?"

I remember watching a movie with the kids when they were a lot younger, a movie called *Pollyanna*, and she was so full of life and fun.

This minister in the movie, he was a pretty negative type of guy.

He said: "Until I met you I always looked for the bad in people . . . now you have shown me to look for the good."

It's so important.

We search for role models because very few of us are perfect but we should always look for the good and be smart enough to see the things we don't like and make sure they don't become part of us.

From time to time, I get the odd letter when one of my star players drifts off the track and the general comment is they're not very good role models. To me, though, they're only showing all the imperfections of the rest of us and I think it's a bit sad because we grab a sports star, put him or her on a pedestal and make out they're some ideal form of human being.

When I picked Gene Miles and, later, Allan Langer to captain the Broncos a major influence was not what they said but what they did.

I want role models to lead our club by their actions, on and off the field.

The thing I know is every young player coming to our club looks at how Allan Langer and the other senior players conduct themselves and I know if I have bad role models then I'm going to have a lot of problems with my future stars.

Again, the younger player doesn't just strut up to Allan Langer to tell him: "I'm watching you . . . I admire you."

But he is, and he does. Every move.

The one quality I have always sought in a person is the willingness to stand up for something, just make a stand. Be relied upon, a guy who'll stick in the tough times.

> **The one quality I have always sought in a person is the willingness to stand up for something, just make a stand.**

Perhaps you will never face tough times together but I still like to have that confidence. No-one who doesn't fit that bill has ever had any influence on my life.

Take my uncle, Eddie Brosnan. He played football, played for Australia. He was at this function, and he didn't mind a drink, Eddie, a very tough man.

Eddie wasn't in this argument but his friend was. He walked over and said to this other guy: "If you want to take on my friend, you have to take me on, too."

The guy said it had nothing to do with Eddie, who shook his head: "It has everything to do with me. He is my friend. If he's wrong, I'm wrong."

You have a lot of great mates but they're not necessarily role models.

Eddie Brosnan was like that all of his life, so rock solid. I remember one night I was in a car, saw his, and followed it. He thought I was the police, so he stopped and I stopped behind him, thinking he wanted to talk to me. He wanted to talk all right even though he didn't know it was me.

He stormed up to challenge what he thought was the police following him.

"Oh it's you, boy," he said. "I was going to go on the front foot."

It wasn't that he didn't respect the police — he was a policeman himself — it's just that he challenged situations he saw as wrong.

It's a characteristic I've always looked for. You have a lot of great mates but they're not necessarily role models. The problem is, whether it's dance or gymnastics, football or politics, many people find their role model and become totally obsessed with them when they should not be so narrow minded and instead look at other people and other walks of life. We must always remain ourselves.

Sure, take a little piece here, a little bit there, and blend them into your own personality but never too many bits, not so that you become a false commodity. Someone else.

I was very much influenced by our military history, particularly as a kid. Just reading. Lining up down the main street on Anzac Day, it had a powerful effect on me.

I'd ask myself if I had been born in a different era, how would I have handled war? These men, they were no different to us. They questioned themselves, too, it's just they had no choice but to find the answers.

Anzac Day, to me, glorifies nothing. It's just a reminder, an insight.

Growing up, whenever I was asked to do something hard, mostly physically but sometimes mentally, and I felt exhausted, that I just couldn't do it, I'd think of the soldiers, their hardships.

Somehow, it gave me strength, the strength not to give up. As you read this article you might ask yourself one question. A simple question. What type of role model are you?

OUR MODEST HERO MAL – FROM CADET TO FEARLESS LEADER

JUNE 18, 1994

When we say goodbye, it's true, a part of us dies.

The first time I saw Mal Meninga was as a 16-year-old cadet at the Queensland Police Academy, where I worked as an instructor.

In Brisbane the other night, at his testimonial dinner, we farewelled the Australian captain, now 33 going on rugby league immortality.

I spoke about Big Mal, as he is affectionately known to us, in two parts: first, the football player, and then the man.

No way did I set out to make Mal sound holier than thou, and while he is not without fault, he was smart in that if he made a mistake, he never repeated it. I looked for a silly story to tell about him, and actually went to Gary Belcher, Peter Jackson and other friends in the search, but, no, we have nothing on Big Mal. He simply didn't do silly things.

Unlike many players, he never had to pump up for a game or for life. To him, even at 16, football always came naturally. We had a big match at the Academy, and it was 20 minutes to kickoff when the superintendent walked in. We were all a little on edge and I remember thinking: "I better make this a decent speech."

All the players were there except for Mal, so I went looking for him. And there he was, out the back hoeing into the six rounds of chicken sandwiches his aunty had carefully prepared for him. Welcome Chicken George.

When I first met him, he was quiet, respectful, a retiring young man yet still powerfully motivated and confident about himself, and the person in the big seat at the testimonial was nothing more or less.

In that time at the Academy one thing stood out. At the end of his second year, Mal told me he was resigning his cadetship and going home to the Sunshine Coast to play football for Palmwoods. Lord, why? He said he didn't want to leave the police force, or the Academy, but that his father had accepted a coaching job up there and was short on players.

> When I first met him, he was quiet, respectful, a retiring young man yet still powerfully motivated and confident about himself.

Out of love and respect for his father, he had decided to do what he could to help, no matter the price.

At the beginning of 1979, his dad no longer coaching, Mal returned to the police academy and kicked off his senior playing career with my club Southern Suburbs, a 16-year path which would never see him play a reserve grade game.

The greatest tribute a sportsperson can receive is the simple one of being a winner. Look at this career, and marvel at a winner — 13 playoff series, 10 grand finals, State of Origin from the beginning, a member and finally captain of three Kangaroo tours — all victorious in Ashes campaigns — under coaches Frank Stanton, Don Furner and Bob Fulton.

And a great team man too. A "team man" is someone who makes those around him play better than they thought they could. He had that ability to give others confidence in themselves to get the job done.

I believe his greatest test came with his greatest disappointments when he suffered that original broken arm and the three recurring cracks. Two years it subtracted from his footballing life, the magnitude of the man highlighted each time he came back, more determined again.

Mal's had more than his share of knockers and it's ironical he's to play his 32nd Origin game on Monday night and still the knockers, the same guys who were barking in 1980, are saying he shouldn't be there.

Next year, when he's not there, those same cretins will be crying: "Bring back Mal."

How he's handled the criticism has been one of his successes, the way he's turned it around and made it a positive, forever striking back on to centre stage and performing.

The greatest game I saw him play was for Canberra against Eastern Suburbs in the 1987 preliminary final.

Mal had been out for five months, busted, and done very little training, yet he was outstanding, setting up a try for Gary Belcher and scoring another from short range straight over the top of Easts hooker David Trewhella.

A coach in the stands doesn't feel for the opposition too often but I felt for Trewhella that day, lying there like a small animal run over by a large truck on the Bruce Highway. They took him to the head bin, and he never came back.

Never.

Speed, strength, skill, temperament — I was always in awe of Mal. That last pass to Mark Coyne to clinch Origin I this year, it wasn't until I looked at it on video that I realised he was one of the few players capable of executing it. A moment earlier, a moment later, Coyne doesn't score. One moment somehow showcased 16 years of training.

I hardly ever remember criticising him. Sure, he had his bad games but not once did he set out to fail. Seeking attention was as foreign to him as not putting in at training or the word "problem".

> **Speed, strength, skill, temperament — I was always in awe of Mal.**

I'm more proud, though, of what he achieved as a person. Mal was always going to play for Australia, no problems. The pat on the back, instead, is for the way he handled it all.

When he came home from the 1983 Kangaroo tour after being very successful, we approached Barry Maranta who was looking after various sports people, including Greg Chappell, about managing Mal.

Barry came out and spoke to him at great length, finally walking up to me and saying: "He's a remarkable young man but forget about anyone managing him. Mal Meninga's too honest and too loyal to be *managed*."

Humility, that's the word, and even when I coached sides against him I never wanted to see him fail. In 1990, he had scored a cruncher against the Broncos in the playoffs, and I remember saying to Peter Jackson at halftime: "What happened?"

Jacko threw his hands in the air and replied: "Coach, I called 'touch' but Big Mal just wouldn't stop."

It is not coincidence he is captain of Canberra, Queensland and Australia and a billboard of respect for his peers and the decision-makers.

Something is dying right now because we know there will never be another quite like him. Still, something lives on in that we will compare and remember him long after others are forgotten.

Thanks, Big Mal, and enjoy the chicken sandwiches.

JACK GIBSON —
IN A LEAGUE OF HIS OWN

JULY 30, 1994

We were at Brisbane Brothers in the late winter of '79, a week short of playing the preliminary final, when club boss Jack Astill strutted up. "Can I do anything for you?" said Jack.

I nodded, explaining that, yeah there was one thing I'd love to have — Jack Gibson spend a day with our players.

When Jack Gibson walked into Brothers that week I was like a kid in a toyshop.

For so long I'd studied this great coach from afar, and, suddenly, here he was in person, with such wonderful humility and knowledge of life.

After just one working day he made you feel as if you had known him all your life, that you could trust him and that he trusted you.

He was leaving, and I said: "Jack, if we win on Sunday I've got this film to show them next week."

Dry as you like, he turned and replied: "When I'm gone, Wayne, ya gunna need somethin' special."

And he was right. We won the preliminary final but got belted the next week in the grand final. The film, obviously, was not special enough — what we really needed was another day with Jack Gibson.

To me, he is the basis of the biggest influence the game has known. I never played under him, never coached under him and have always felt envious of those who had the privilege.

Through the '70s and '80s, the most dominant people in the game were Jack Gibson and, later, Warren Ryan.

Jack made everyone realise the importance of the coach. Until Jack Gibson, coaches were second-class citizens. All the recognition pointed to the players and officials and, while I wouldn't mind if that still happened, Jack somehow made the coach a part of the team.

To me, he is the basis of the biggest influence the game has known.

Before Jack, and the old fellas will tell you this, the coach just had to make sure the balls were pumped up for training.

"Hey guys, who we playin' today?"

Wests.

"Hah, see ya at 'alf time — we'll kick those guys' butts."

Jack Gibson changed all that, and I'm a fulltime coach today through him in more ways than one. He was the first fulltime coach, now there's not a part-timer.

And it was Jack who gave us the great team concepts, introducing the coordinator (Ron Massey — Jack's right-hand man all the way through and whose influence on the game can never be overestimated), the fitness guy (Mick Souter) and the sports medicine guy (Alf Richards) when sports medicine was in its infancy.

The first to concentrate on weight-training, so significant in the modern game. Pre-season camps, motivational films . . . in '74, when Paul Broughton was coaching us at Brothers, he got this film called *The Second Effort*. I remember Paul saying, "This comes from Jack Gibson." It was about Vince Lombardi and a salesman and to this day it is the best film I have seen.

Jack found it in America and I've heard some of his friends say he thinks of himself as a reborn American, with those one-liners and such.

That's another thing, the video — Jack introduced the video to rugby league and it has had a greater impact on our game than just about anything or anyone.

The video made us all better coaches. Jack, he kicked off with black-and-white film, recording players' mistakes. In the old days, when we threw a bad pass we all had such a bad memory but when the coach brought it up on Tuesday night you couldn't remember it happening, and, basically, it was his word against yours. Jack could prove it in black-and-white and, together, you could fix it.

It was Jack who formed the players' association because he always believed in the players having a voice and respectability in the game.

Just recently I noted he was criticised in one of the papers. I thought that a pity, and again wondered how many people understand or comprehend his achievements.

Discipline, he gave us that too, convincing his players there was no room for cheap shots.

Black-tie dinners for players, tackle counts . . . there's a good yarn here. Harry Bath was quite a successful coach himself and when Jack introduced tackle counts, old Harry said he had no use for them, that he could tell how a player was tackling without keeping count. Some time later, Harry replaced a prominent player mid-match and back in the rooms, when asked why by a journo, replied: "His tackle count was too low."

Jack got rid of selectors. Once I heard him asked what he thought of selectors? "Aren't they tiny things in the gearbox of a car?"

In his early coaching days even Jack had to put up with selectors and at St George, they tell me, they'd get to Graeme Langlands and the selectors obviously would want Langlands in the team but Jack would fight against it.

> **He has this presence that makes you sense he wouldn't fail you and you wouldn't want to fail him.**

Finally, he'd give in, and they'd move on to another established international and again he'd fight it. Then it would happen: Jack would want some unknown kid in the team and he'd say, "Come on fellas, I gave you Langlands and Smith, ya gotta give me one back."

They labelled him, unfairly, a defensive coach but I doubt Jack ever told Russell Fairfax, Mark Harris, Ian Schubert, Steve Ella, Eric Grothe, Arthur Beetson or Brett Kenny not to run.

He taught us that winners didn't just hang around the sideline waiting for the ball and of tackling drills previously unknown. When they brought him up to coach Queensland Country I remember one of our greatest coaches, Duncan Thompson, just before his death, watching these tackling drills.

Old Duncan walked over and shook Jack by the hand, saying: "I'm very impressed — in all my years I have never seen players being coached in defence."

This week, every kid in every park training to play rugby league was touched, in some way, by Jack Gibson.

Even before I began coaching I used to love watching him on TV, I just used to laugh and laugh. I loved the way he handled reporters, and the way he made nothing sound really something.

He has this presence that makes you sense he wouldn't fail you and you wouldn't want to fail him. You want to please him because you know he's not lying to you, not trying to con you.

Jack figured coaching was done through the week, and if he had nothing to say just before the match or at halftime, he said nothing. The only halftime speech he ever remembered as a player was when it was pouring rain, mud everywhere, from the field to the dressing rooms, and this coach, dressed in a beautiful suit and totally upset with his players' tackling, dived bang into the mud, screaming: "This is the way you tackle."

I like what he stands for, the honesty bit and the team, the way he does things for people who can do nothing for him.

When the Broncos were looking for their first coach, he recommended me for the job.

And when all is said and done, I find it hard to criticise Jack Gibson.

Talking heads inject code with style

July 4, 1994

When I was growing up in rugby league sure there were a lot of great guys but the footballer handed the microphone at the function was usually the one who'd had a few too many drinks.

His image was not that good and when he'd speak not only would he be embarrassed but also the public.

"Aah," he'd say. "I hate speaking in public."

He'd pause, and add: "Bear with me, aah . . ." Anyway, you know the story.

One of the aspects I'm most proud of in the modern game is the image projected by recently retired players.

I remember an article Ray Price once wrote regarding Bob Lindner at Parramatta, whingeing about Bob turning up to training in a BMW.

Price argued rugby league was a working man's game and that its competitors should be seen hurtling down main streets in FJ Holdens, preferably, I suspect, tucking into meat pies at the lights.

At the time I thought what he said and the image he obviously pushed demonstrated a wrong, a lack of imagination. The players of yesterday, you see, if they were seen to be getting ahead, achieving, they were viewed under a different light.

Put simply, they were said to be "up themselves".

To hell they were.

Today I look at Peter Sterling, at Paul Vautin, Peter Jackson, Gary Belcher and Steve Roach and wonder: "What are you driving fellas? I hope it's the very best."

Sterlo I've had a little to do with and have no doubts he would have been a wonderful player to coach, with his commitment, preparation and vision.

> **These guys, they're not afraid to take their personalities everywhere they go, and to everyone's enjoyment.**

And it's the same when he's behind the microphone, as good as anyone I've heard, particularly his knowledge of the game. It has to do with the way he gets across the most complicated point in the most simple manner.

The way Peter Sterling talks about the game is the way he played it.

Same with Paul Vautin. Fatty was funny as a player and those wisecracks you see and hear on the box are simply an extension of that.

These guys, they're not afraid to take their personalities everywhere they go, and to everyone's enjoyment.

One of the things I most enjoy about coaching is the not-so serious side, the way players, past and present, laugh at themselves. They see the fun in life and don't take it too seriously.

Look at Action Jackson.

Peter Jackson, again, he's retired from footy and fitting straight into TV and radio, still so full of energy. That's the way he played it, his style reflected in cliches, funny stories and, at times, corny jokes.

Jacko, like Allan Langer and Kevin Walters, is smart in that while he is quick-witted by nature he knows when the joke has finished . . . when the fun stops and it's time to work.

His is a double-act with wife Siobhan. Rarely have I seen a better suited couple than Peter and Siobhan.

They not only make other people laugh, but each other, and now that Peter's not playing their parties can carry on beyond the once curfew of nine o'clock the next morning.

Gary Belcher is more like Sterlo in that he is a great analyst of the game but different to Fatty and Jacko.

"Badge" was the kid at school who never got the cuts. All the times I trained and coached him, whenever someone would be up to something in good fun, if not always good enough in other areas, Badge would be in the background egging them on.

The way he picks up quickly and responds to other people's comments is reflective of his footballing brain.

Blocker Roach? Here is a Blue always welcomed in Queensland where he does a lot of public speaking.

Queenslanders like Blocker because he's a bit of a rogue and has never pretended to be something he wasn't.

He played it tough, wouldn't hide and he's the same as a commentator — capable of coming out with some absolute clangers.

When he does you have to remember he was a front-rower and front-rowers are walking clangers.

One night as guest speaker I heard him give his then coach, who will remain nameless, a terrible hammering.

Later I walked up and said: "Block, what happens if your speech gets back to the coach?"

"What can he do to me?" he growled straight back.

I didn't say anything more but remembered thinking it was a fair comment, that when you've packed into the front row against the toughest players in the world, how is a little Sydney coach going to hurt you?

> **One of the things I most enjoy about coaching is the not-so-serious side, the way players, past and present, laugh at themselves.**

Prop forwards everywhere owe Blocker Roach and I know Newcastle's Paul Harragon, for one, is following him into the media.

But I still wonder whether TV executives missed out on the biggest star of all — Big Sam Backo.

Sure Big Sam would need just a little voice training but he's always stood out, from the playing field to the stands.

Straight to the point, is our Sam.

No-one could forget his celebrated comments after State of Origin matches. Walking off once a Channel Nine microphone was pushed into his face as he was asked how he'd pulled up?

"I'm f . . . ed," said Sam.

Another time, after a Queensland series win, the question was how his relatives back home would be celebrating. "Oh," said Sam, "they'd be on the piss."

Big Sam's the only footballer in the world who's "PC joint" is still playing up. Every other footballer hurts his "AC joint" but not Sam.

A night after he'd been badly smashed up in a match I visited him in hospital.

"Oh coach," he said as I walked in, "the doctors just did an autopsy on me."

I said: "Sam, you're the first man in history who's ever been brave enough to talk about it — in fact, you just might be the first to have lived through one."

Still, I prefer "autopsy" to "aah".

Cheeky rogues,
Bad losers . . . just like the coach

April 9, 1994

They're the Danny De Vitos of rugby league, and while no coach resembles Big Arnie, we need close relationships, understandings, with our halfbacks — in a way, we have to be *TWINS*.

The halfback is the most dominant player in the game — the money man, the bacon man — and he's got to be an extension of the coach. He's got to think like the coach. He's got to spend more time with the coach, have the same feel for things.

I spent a week with the Denver Broncos in the NFL, with the great John Elway. Those quarterbacks, they're treated like gods, the way everybody talks about them, the staff, the other players, the kids with the autograph books.

Elway's a big fellow, a lovely guy, too. We had a couple of conversations and I watched him train. He must be 6ft 2in (188cm), Elway, and the way he moved, you'd probably play him at lock instead of halfback.

Quarterbacks, they need a great throwing arm, and again like halfbacks, great vision. When to pass, when to hold, what option to take.

I remember showing Denver a video of our Broncos playing, and apart from getting excited about the lack of padding and the body contact, one player caught their attention. After just a few minutes, I think it was Elway who said: "That guy — the No. 6 — he's pretty smart, isn't he? Looks like he really controls the game for you."

The No. 6 was Wally Lewis. I said "Yeah, that's a fair comment."

There's been the odd exception in our game, the five-eighth who's dominated. Terry Lamb at Canterbury, Cliff Lyons has been a wonderful player at Manly, and at State of Origin level Lewis dominated until Alf (Allan Langer) came along. Lewis led Queensland with Mark Murray at halfback being a wonderful foil for him, always prepared to take a lesser role.

> **Building a side from scratch, he's the first guy I want, the cheeky one.**

But with the most successful teams of the '80s and '90s, generally it's been the halfbacks. The Mortimers and Sterlings. Greg Alexander and Ricky Stuart.

Building a side from scratch, he's the first guy I want, the cheeky one. There's a personality required to play this position. Because of the size he has to give away, he's got to have great confidence — it's the one position they can never doubt themselves. He's got to have a lot of fun in him.

Alfie, the first time I saw him, so cheeky and full of fun. Nothing worried him, but two things worried me about him. His size, he was just so small, 62kg. Secondly, his defence certainly wasn't what it is today. Outside of that, he had all the attributes and to his credit, he's improved his defence so much.

I find a lot of guys suffer the small man syndrome. Alfie's got no syndrome at all. At no stage of his life has size been a question in his mind. Never a factor, such a positive person. If he lacks anything, it's just the hunger sometimes. I know if he's on his game, he'll take the rest of us with him. If he's off his game, we can all go down.

The same thing was highlighted at Canberra last year when Ricky Stuart was injured. Lamb at Canterbury. Look what Jason Taylor's done for North Sydney. Norths are probably putting in no more effort, training no harder. And take nothing from Noel Goldthorpe at Saints, the way he steers them around the park.

Regardless of their ability, though, they can be no better than the guys up the front allow them to be. If the guys from the front row to the back row are not performing, the halfback's restricted.

With the exception of Tommy Raudonikis and probably Manly's Geoff Toovey at the moment, there's no halfback physically able to take on an attack one-out.

Jason Taylor at Norths, with an exceptionally tough pack in front of him — undoubtedly he thought about that before switching from Wests.

Tommy Raudonikis? Oh, tough. I had great admiration for Tommy Raudonikis. He didn't know how to lose. People bring up the larrikin in Tommy but I'd be optimistic enough to think had I got him young enough I could have kept him straight. Tommy's my type of player, of halfback. It's true there was a lot of rogue in Tommy, like Alf, but if managed properly, it's controllable.

Barry Muir? The best pass I've ever seen. We had a game of touch a couple of years ago and Barry reminded me of the old school.

Billy Smith, same story. Steve Mortimer, I used to love watching Steve Mortimer play. Great speed. He probably doesn't fit the rogue category, but the way he organised that '85 State of Origin series. His passion and drive won them (NSW) that series. That match at the SCG, his leadership.

Sterling, he was the complete general, in the Wally Lewis category. I reckon he would have made coaching that much easier. I like him. You hear his comments on TV, he talks like a coach. If anyone's genuinely interested in rugby league he'll gain more tips in one night listening to Sterling than he'll get off all the Winfield Cup coaches combined in a month.

I find a lot of guys suffer the small man syndrome. Alfie's got no syndrome at all.

In 1987 I was at Canberra and we made the grand final after being mid-field halfway through the year — winning some, losing some. With six games to go, we made the decision to put Ivan Henjak at halfback. From that point we were always going to be there.

We didn't train any harder, didn't play any harder, but with Ivan directing play and the players, we simply played better. Canberra had finished 12th or 13th the year before. With eight games to go in '87, we played Parramatta and Peter Sterling won the game for them. I remember sitting there, this great frustration, the way he dictated to us. That was the day I made the decision — we had to get a halfback.

We have no successor for Alf at the Broncos, our next-best option being five-eighth Kevvie Walters who I'd rate in the top five halfbacks in the game.

I know what I'm looking for — a bit of a rogue, someone who's cheeky, and when I say jump doesn't necessarily ask how high? But most importantly, someone the others will follow, who detests losing.

If Alf has one major factor above everything else, he's a poor loser.

That, alone, almost makes us *TWINS*.

MAY THE BEST
TEAM WIN – I JUST HOPE IT'S MAL'S

SEPTEMBER 24, 1994

This is the day. Why people in rugby league get up, why they lie down. State of Origins, they're great, but grand finals they're not.

It's the one day in your coaching life where the feeling is somehow relaxed, strangely.

The great challenge is behind you, that being just to get there.

And the week leading up . . . it too is an absolute pleasure. The enthusiasm, the closeness, that's the greatest thing. The atmosphere in the rooms, even at training. The kids, the parents, the grandparents. The media. The radio stations at the ground doing their outside broadcasts.

It's a carnival.

Of course I feel a sadness about the Broncos not being there again but am realistic enough to realise there is no mortgage on anything in life.

The Broncos only have the Broncos to blame for not being there, and we realise other players and other clubs work just as hard.

Canberra and Canterbury, they've done it all fairly.

I had a friend ring yesterday wanting to put some money on the game and I honestly couldn't tip him either way.

It's just so close, but I have no doubt the Lomax factor is important. The last time Canterbury played Canberra the Bulldogs really got into him. When the opposition think that highly of a player you immediately sense how team-mates rate the same player. John Lomax, Canberra's go-forward forward, is obviously a gun and a sorry loss for the Raiders.

But Canterbury could be 10 points in front with 10 minutes to go and still be a long way off being a sure thing.

> **Canterbury must live up to their name. They have to be Bulldogs, don't they?**

That's the problem with playing Canberra — at no stage are they beaten.

Like any grand final side, their strengths are all over the park. Canberra play that stacked-up defence that can so easily intimidate, and they scramble well. In other words, if the line is broken you can just about put the rent on someone still turning up to make the tackle.

In attack, they have a halfback in Ricky Stuart who really controls it. There's his kicking game, of course. The Raiders ride on the back of it, minimising mistakes. That's where they came unstuck against Canterbury last time around, making uncharacteristic errors.

Individually, there's Mal Meninga, Ken Nagas, Brett Mullins, Steve Walters, Laurie Daley, Stuart, David Furner . . . most of their guys can pull out something special.

Against Norths it was Mullins from dummy-half, against Canterbury it was Furner into a hole with just 50 seconds on the clock.

The Raiders will be probing, trying things all day and putting Canterbury under constant and enormous pressure.

Canterbury must live up to their name. They have to be Bulldogs, don't they?

This '94 side has some real surprises. The wingers Daryl Halligan and Jason Williams, one guy kicking well and playing well and the other guy . . . that Williams, when he's got the ball no-one knows what he's going to do. I doubt he knows. He just does it. And it works.

McCracken in the centres, he's aggressive. He's going to scare hell out of the other guys. None of them want to be standing in tackles doing the fancy stuff when he's around. And even when he's got the ball there's no fancy footwork or anything. Just bang, crash, wallop.

McCracken's centre partner Steven Hughes, they tell me he's got one foot on the Kangaroo tour plane. Sounds to me like this is the luckiest guy in the world. When I heard it I immediately recalled Bullfrog Moore, a few years ago, telling a player who was leaving Canterbury for another club: "Son, you'll never play again for Australia." At the time I remember thinking, come on, Bullfrog, you're kidding, you haven't that much power. But now, when I think of it, that guy never played again for Australia. Bullfrog wasn't kidding at all.

Terry Lamb? A friend recently said to me, and I think he got it right, that Terry Lamb's most dangerous when he *hasn't* got the ball. By that, he was talking about Lamb's ability to turn up in places he really shouldn't be — usually over the try line. He can be tackled, on the ground and get out of it, jump up and take the backup pass that wins the game or turns the game or whatever.

Polla-Mounter, he's aggressive and tough, Dymock, a wonderful buy. He'll worry Canberra.

Dean Pay's one of those mixture players in that some have a wrap on him and others don't. I'm in the wrap category, it's mainly because of the things he can do with the football.

Jason Smith has so much flair, he's great, and the little hooker Jason Hetherington, he'll only get better. He's a bit of a hero, that kid.

To Marty Bella. Only his mother could love him. The man's got a receding hairline so he goes and buys himself a crew cut. That's Marty. He's been around a long time, had a few clubs, yet it's his first grand final.

> **We'll all miss seeing his playing ability, but more than anything I will miss his statesman-like approach to, and standing in, the game.**

I really wanted to see the Maroons win this year's Origin series for Mal Meninga, but sadly it didn't come.

Early in the week I had this image of Cronin and Price after the '86 grand final, and two days later I saw the same thing photographed in a newspaper. They were on their victory lap, retired. It was all so fitting and emotional.

I know Mal Meninga well enough to say he would have wanted the Origin series, the grand final and a clean sweep Kangaroo tour, as captain, in his final year.

No one has greater desire, and this desire has had a tremendous influence on Canberra, and that's not taking anything from the coach or anyone else.

Look back just a week, to the Norths match, and when the game got tough and tight, Big Mal strode into the arena.

The game Mal Meninga came into in 1979 has had its ups and downs, like an elevator just lately, but he has remained constant, a credit to the game.

I can't remember him ever having to apologise for anything he has said in public. A lot of players will mouth off, then blame the reporter for misquoting him. Mal never blamed a reporter for that, maybe because he never mouthed off.

We'll all miss seeing his playing ability, but more than anything I will miss his statesman-like approach to, and standing in, the game.

Mal Meninga never stopped feeling he owed rugby league. When it comes down to a grand final, you just want the best team to win, understanding the hardships and heartbreaks both sides have suffered.

No one wants to see any other influence on the game.

So may the best team win. I just hope it's Mal's.

wayne
B E N N E T T

ON MATES

---

*A mate to me is someone who will
not let you down. You trust him, he trusts
you and you can both be relied upon.*

A LIFE'S CREED CAN BE SUMMED UP WITH ONE SIMPLE WORD: MATESHIP

AUGUST 12, 1995

This is about mateship. After last week's win against Wests, I said the Broncos were playing for each other again.

It was an off-the-top-of-the-head statement, something I hadn't thought about, but it had been obvious right through the game it was a fact.

This week, with the anniversary of the end of the Pacific War — the radio reports, the television and the papers — I got to thinking about mates.

What they mean, and why mates mean so much.

A mate to me is someone who will not let you down. You trust him, he trusts you and you can both be relied upon.

Recently I read somewhere — and it's right — for the friendship of two, the patience of one is necessary.

Mateship is the reason we do things for one another, in family, in sport and in business.

Regardless of how much pay you get, we all need mates, without that common bond we wouldn't achieve nor reach any real heights.

Again using the Broncos as an example, if we are to be a force in this year's playoffs it will be because of mateship.

I know this because we won in '92 and '93 and the most dominant factor was mateship.

With your family, mateship can certainly have an impact. More than once my wife is asked the question: Who comes first? My mates or her?

We've all been asked a similar question, and I just say when asked: "It's a hard question."

When I told her I was going to mention that in this article, she said: "To be honest, Wayne, I'm not that stupid — I don't have to ask."

I've just watched a documentary and it had a profound effect on me. It was called *SANDAKAN*, and was about the atrocities in Borneo during the Second World War: the forced march and the killing of Australian soldiers.

Four survivors are still alive, and the documentary focused on one of those old soldiers, a good bloke who told how he lost his best mate.

They had spent so much time together; firstly in action, then through the prisoner-of-war camps, did the death marches together, and just about made it to the end of the war when his mate was killed. He kept calling him "my mate". He said for the past 45 years he has thought of his mate. Every day.

I once saw a guy named Joe Greene, a Pittsburgh Steeler linesman of the 1970s. He was being interviewed and said there were many times he didn't want to pay the price personally on the football field. He said there's no price he wouldn't pay for his team-mates, however.

There are many times in our lives when we are inclined to let ourselves down but don't, not because of ourselves but because of our mates. In many ways they make us what we are. I've thought about it a lot.

There doesn't have to be danger or adversity around for mateship to shine through. It can be in everyday things, and often I use these everyday things in talks with the players. Mateship

Mateship can extend simply by putting yourself out, by putting your mate first.

can extend simply by putting yourself out, by putting your mate first. They trudge in from training, thirsty as hell, and the first guy gets to the first cup of water.

You see this guy, knowing how thirsty he is, pick up the cup, turn around and hand it on. He's a mate.

I asked a friend what he thought about mateship and he said it was the thing he'd missed most in the past 10 years. He'd been an underground miner and had had some great mates down there before advancing in the company to a job way above any of that.

He now works alone. His mates are still there but he just doesn't see them often.

It's a great loss for sportsmen when they retire, the thing they really miss.

After we'd beaten Wests I saw my players at the airport really enjoying each other's company. I just stood there thinking, for a couple of them, it's not all that long before their careers end. I afterwards reminded them of mateship, how it's never to be taken for granted. I showed them this; something I first heard when read at the funeral of the father of one of my former players:

I've travelled down some lonely roads, both crooked tracks and straight. And I've learnt life's creed. Summed it up in one word — MATE.

I'm thinking back across the years (a thing I do lately) and these words stick between my ears: "You've got to have a mate."

My mind goes back to '43, to slavery and hate. When man's one chance to stay alive depended on his mate.

You'd slip and slither through the mud and curse your rotten fate.

But then you'd hear a quiet word — "Don't drop your bundle, mate."

And though it's all so long ago this truth I have to state — a man doesn't know what lonely means till he's lost his mate.

If there's a life that follows this, if there's a golden gate, the words that I want to hear are just "Good onya mate."

And when I've left the driver's seat, and handed in the plates, I'll tell old Peter at the door, I've come to join my mates.

Just one last thing: Have you got a mate?

STRAIGHT
FROM THE FARMER'S MOUTH

These two guys are travelling together when they suddenly spy a bear.

Before the bear sees them one man races to a tree, climbs up and hides. The other man isn't so nimble, can't escape and throws himself down and plays "dead".

The bear saunters up and sniffs around. Finally, the bear whispers something into the "dead" man's ear.

Climbing down, the first traveller asks what the bear said? His companion replies: "He told me never to travel with someone who'll desert me at the first sign of danger."

My farmer mate would either lie down beside me or find the strength to carry me high into the tree.

This week I was at his place again, chasing cows, and he couldn't wait to ask: "Who's been writing Ken Arthurson's lines?"

As if I know.

"He's certainly got through plenty of bagging. Do you think Graham Richardson's been writing the lines?" my mate asked.

Again, as if I know.

"You know, the way they're conducting their campaign against Super League, it's a carbon copy of Keating's last election strategy."

How so?

"Well, the Libs had all the policies, Labor nil, and Keating just bagged the hell out of everything. Super League have all the plans, the Australian Rugby League none, but Senator Graham made one mistake — nobody gets a vote in this little number."

Yeah.

"I couldn't believe the Origin, Kenny clapping for Queensland. Still, he couldn't con the Queensland fans — they booed him regardless."

Yeah.

"What about this loyalty to the ARL I keep reading about?"

"I wouldn't want that type of loyalty."

OK, you win, why?

"It's costing hundreds of millions of dollars."

Hmm.

"Hey, what about when Kenny said rugby league belonged to the people . . . I took that to mean it belongs to me. You and I know it doesn't belong to me, never has, so why shouldn't it be owned by Rupert (Murdoch) instead of Kerry (Packer), Bozo (Bob Fulton) and co.

"I liked that one Kenny said about only family and friends turning up for Canterbury games, because there's at least four clubs loyal to the ARL, where the players' own children refuse to go to matches."

Yeah, and their wives won't even watch the replays.

"What's happened to John Quayle?"

Don't know.

"Do you think John's gone down that mine at Cobar again, got lost? Anyway how's the Mushroom going?"

John Ribot?

"He's in a pretty powerful position, the Mushroom. Reminds me of Margaret Thatcher, how she always said being powerful is like being a lady — if you have to tell people you are, you aren't. With all his so-called visions, is the Mushroom a bit of a dreamer?"

> **"Whatever you do, or dream you can do — begin it."**

That's pretty profound for you farmer, but he is a bit.

"A guy once said: 'Whatever you do, or dream you can do — begin it. Boldness has genius and power and madness in it'."

Holy moly. Profundity No. 2.

"What about Kenny calling Maurice Lindsay, the Pommy boss, *Nero*, sitting up at Cairns in the sunshine while Great Britain burned. I remember when Kenny came home from last year's Kangaroo Tour to put out the fire."

If you had a fire like that one, your place wouldn't be a place any more . . . hey farmer, why are you running away?

"I think I just spied a bear."

I'm not holding my breath.

FULLTIME FOR
A MAN WHO ENRICHED US ALL

AUGUST 5, 1995

I looked at his photo on the front page of *The Australian*, his left eye squinting through those glasses and the red spots on his bald head.

Most of all I looked at his smile.

Fred Daly, more than just a joker, read the headline.

Footballers are different creatures in that nothing usually affects or interests them outside of their own lives.

But it was different at training on Thursday morning, the way they all turned up sad with a good word for a good man gone.

When Kevin Walters, Glenn Lazarus and Ivan Henjak said their bits, that was easily understood.

They all played at Canberra Raiders where Fred was club patron, and when they left he wrote them letters of thanks and best wishes.

Still, Allan Langer never played at Canberra and didn't need a letter to be touched by Fred Daly.

I never spent more than a few hours with him, probably not enough to be worthy of actually *knowing* him, yet I feel I do.

When I went to coach Canberra in '87 I hadn't been involved in what you call the Big League.

I just got to meet him as you meet people.

Obviously, I knew about his political career but was still a young man, and like most young men didn't care too much about politics.

One of the benefits, the great joys about being involved in sport is the opportunity to meet special people.

Fred Daly, more than most, had a wonderful presence about him.

Through his own humility he made you feel so humble, so comfortable.

You could always be yourself with him.

He never sought a favour, just mateship, and he smiled a lot, even after the worst of defeats.

Once Fred explained to me how he'd been heavily involved at Newtown as club patron and sitting member.

After every losing season and every losing game at Newtown, Fred had always made a point of seeking out the opposition's chairman or coach and apologising for his team's performance.

The funny thing was, when Newtown began winning in the late '70s he had been apologising for so long he found himself apologising for winning.

He told me two yarns I'd never before heard.

I hear them most every day now: how things got so bad, Newtown won the toss once and did a lap of honour.

Then the one about the captain saying, "Okay, take up your normal positions" and everyone going behind the goalposts.

The last time I saw him was in April down in Canberra where the Raiders gave us a fair old hiding.

Through his own humility he made you feel so humble, so comfortable.

He came into the Broncos room, smiling, shook my hand and apologised.

When I was about to leave the Canberra coaching job to return to Brisbane and the Broncos, more and more I was being invited to do public speaking.

It's part of coaching, being able to speak in public and everyone told me there was no finer speaker than Fred.

So I asked him for a half-hour of his time and he invited me to his house.

We spent a couple of hours alone, and I still go through those wonderful notes.

Understanding my public persona he gave me a tip on the best way to get an audience onside with a humorous remark at the very beginning.

"Wayne," he said, "one I've used all over Australia: after they've introduced you, particularly if it's long-winded, take a long pause and open with — 'After that introduction, I can't wait to hear myself speak'."

People like Fred made this game great.

When I left he gave me this book, his book, entitled *From Curtin to Hawke* and I have it with me right now.

On the inside cover he has penned: "Best wishes and pleasant memories of your time in Canberra and your grand contribution to the Raiders' success in the greatest game of all. Fred Daly."

People like Fred made this game great.

He never once told a team how to play, or what was wrong.

Always totally unobtrusive.

In the rooms the players look for that kindness, sincerity and consistency.

Through this column I have an opportunity to say what all sporting people are feeling, how Fred Daly made us all better people with a shake of the hand and a smile. Then he'd be gone.

To the very end, he never once outstayed his welcome.

PLOUGHING BETWEEN THE LINES

AUGUST 13, 1994

My farmer mate works from five in the morning to seven at night and never has time to read the paper. Not cover to cover, at least.

As I mentioned at the start of the season, his place is my retreat. The cows don't cheer or boo. The fences don't stop at the horizon, they just keep going.

Like many in the bush, my mate's been knocked around badly by the drought. He says that to be a farmer you need the heart of Phar Lap and a brain the size of a pea.

His courage and never-say-die attitude blend to produce a toughness not always seen on the football field. Give him two inches of rain and he'll be smiling again, despite the roughest of times.

We don't talk about the League bosses, or the Bronco bosses or the bosses' bosses because, as he is apt to say, "You never know a man until you've eaten a bag of flour with him." He means that you really don't understand someone until you've lived with them, faced some adversity together.

Invariably, whether we're milking the cows or building a new fence, talk turns to football.

"How do you think Alan Cann's been feeling lately?" he asked me.

"Really good," I said. "He's back playing, enjoying his footy."

"But he got four weeks for a head-high," said my farmer mate. "I get to see a bit of football on TV and in the past month I've seen enough good head-highs to make me wonder how a bloke like Alan

Cann must be feeling? I'm watching that game the other night. Canberra and Canterbury, and I see this bloke get lifted. Looked pretty dangerous to me. How's Kerrod Walters feeling? Old Kerrod, another thing he must be wondering about is why his apology to the League didn't work. You know, for those things he said about the judiciary.

> **You really don't understand someone until you've lived with them, faced some adversity together.**

"That Phil Gould's obviously much better at this apologising caper, and I reckon you should send old Kerrod down to Bondi Junction, just let him sit in the stands and learn."

"Listen mate, you don't understand," I protested.

"Understand what? I see the TV," he said.

"It's just the way the game is," I said.

"I did see you got a bit of good news."

"What's that?" I asked him.

"One of the refs is going to live in England."

"Give me a break," I complained.

"Well, looks like the Broncos are starting to play a bit of football at long last. About bloody time. Even the cows were starting to switch off the telly when they ran on," he said.

"I suppose, mate, we've been through one of those seasons and are left with no-one to blame but ourselves. At times we looked for the easy yards, didn't give enough attention to detail," I replied.

"Looks like you've stopped the rot, anyway," he said.

"Yeah, but it's still extremely fragile," I explained. "The next couple of weeks are obviously vital to us. The attitude's certainly turned. At the beginning of the season players were saying the right things but no-one was providing the action. Now there's less talk and plenty of action.

"What probably started the turnaround was the second half of the World Challenge match against Wigan. We had to give some young guys a shot and this made some of the more established players understand we could probably get the job done without them."

He brought the conversation back to the cows.

"It's like my milkers, I love 'em," he said. "But they get old and they've got to be sold. Hate doing it, mate, but it keeps the herd on its toes. What about all those coaches they've been sackin'? How you feeling?"

"Well, I've had those moments of insecurity but they were years ago," I told him.

"It doesn't do much for the game," he complained. "Everyone says it's a business and I understand that, but surely an employee should be able to last until the end of the year."

I suggested he didn't understand.

"What don't I understand? Someone's got to finish down the line. They can't all be premiers."

"But the club has to be seen to be doing something," I said. "Players can be mediocre, committees can be mediocre, but the coach has got to be doing something."

"Gus (Gould) seems to be the only one who's done any good out of it," he observed. "A juicy new contract and a job at Channel Nine as well."

"You don't understand," I replied.

"Obviously. One thing up here on the farm, I don't have to have any committee meetings. So I don't have to worry," he said.

"Mate, you're beginning to understand," I said.

"If that's *understanding*, I don't want to understand," he said.

I left the farm mentally refreshed. At day's end, the fence is complete and you know that if a single wire is not tightly strung or one post is not dead straight under the spirit level, you're not going to read about it in tomorrow's headlines.

Retiring top dog a special breed

September 16, 1995

We first met — formally, at least — not on any recognised rugby league ground but a world away in Los Angeles.

Queensland had already won the 1987 State of Origin series and were in LA for a fourth match, purely a promotional exercise.

Great controversy clouded the players' availability for the following weekend's competition round, with a number of clubs demanding their representatives jump on a plane early the morning after the match to be home in time for the club games.

Peter Moore's Canterbury Bulldogs demanded louder than all others.

In his role as manager of the New South Wales team, Peter had sat his players up on the front of the plane on the way over, dishing up mineral water and health foods while we Queenslanders, as usual, were up the back of the bus partying.

Even during the stopover in Hawaii, as our celebrations continued, he had special foods delivered to his men, holed up under tight security.

Some clubs had granted their players a few days leave after the LA match and most of the Queenslanders were headed to Las Vegas with all the enthusiasm of those guys in the Oh What A Feeling ads.

Not Tony Currie, though.

Sure Tony was a Maroon and wanted to be with his mates, but when he wasn't playing for Queensland he played for the

Canterbury Bulldogs and, according to Peter Moore, a Bulldogs' place was at home.

Anyway, and predictably, New South Wales won the match and immediately afterwards up walked Tony Currie. No way did he want to fly home. No, he wanted to go to Vegas.

I'm still cheesed off with the performance, but he fronted me regardless.

"Look, I've got a bit of a cork," said Tony, pointing to a leg. "If Bullfrog (as Peter Moore's known affectionately) comes in, can you tell him I can't go home — that I need treatment?"

I said: "Wanna be a great cork to convince Bullfrog."

Tony, looking down and grimacing, replied: "It will be when we're finished with it."

And with that he was off, strutting around the dressing room corner to where Paul Vautin and Trevor Gillmeister awaited him in the showers area. I hear this *thump*, *thump*, *thump*, and agonising screams before

Bullfrog disappeared around the corner for five minutes, or thereabouts, reappearing a broken man.

walking around myself to find Fatty and Gilly punching Tony — at his request, of course — right on the corked area. Within minutes, the guy could barely walk.

I'm back in the main area, perfecting that don't-annoy-me-now look, when in walked Peter Moore.

Obviously my reputation had preceded me, because this was our first official meeting and he still kicked it off with the words: "Don't give me a hassle, Wayne."

What was I going to hassle him about?

"Tony Currie," he said.

I said: "The kid's around there . . . he's no good. He won't be any good to you next weekend."

Bullfrog disappeared around the corner for five minutes, or thereabouts, reappearing a broken man.

"Matey," he said, as he always says, "Matey, he's no good. Can he stay here with you?"

Just then Tony came limping, horribly, around the corner and

Bullfrog gave him one last fatherly tap on the shoulder before leaving.

Today, as Peter Moore pats every Bulldog of the past 20 years on the shoulder with his goodbye as club chief executive, we reflect on one of the game's finest and most imposing reigns.

When Peter took over at Canterbury in 1970 the club, in the previous 20 years, had twice made the semis and played in one grand final. Since? In 25 years, 20 playoff series. That's right, 20. Year after year, coach after coach, player after player. The one thing that remained constant — the front office.

For the Broncos, our year has finished but we realise our greatest strength and future is in our front office.

Long ago I remember Jack Gibson saying that whenever he went anywhere to look at a coaching job, the first thing he looked at was that front office.

Peter Moore leaves the Bulldogs with their well-documented troubles of this season over, behind them, and he leaves it like we all want to leave places — in better shape than when we arrived.

There are many wonderful stories regarding Super League's new worldwide recruitment officer and many people better qualified than I to tell them but bear with me all the same.

When Canterbury won one of those grand finals in the late '80s, '88 I think, a couple of weeks later Allan Langer ran into Peter Moore.

Alfie, being of the cheeky brand, geed up Bullfrog, saying: "How about you? The way you carried on! Doing victory laps, lairising . . ."

Then in '92, when the Broncos won their first premiership, a fax arrived from Bulldogs' headquarters in double quick time. It was addressed to Alf.

Bullfrog would pick the dominant factor in any relationship and hone in.

"How about you?" it said. "The way you carried on! That stupid hat . . ."

He has a relationship with most players from most clubs, not just players either, but most of all he has relationships with Bulldogs.

Pause a moment and remember the players he recruited.

Remember Greg Brentnall, the Mortimers, Chris Anderson . . . and even the players who are no longer there, like Langmack, Darren Smith and David Gillespie.

In recruitment drives, he was always the hardest to beat.

The Broncos wanted Brett Dallas, and we wanted him badly but, sadly, so did Bullfrog and on the day we went to sign him there he was, just minutes after a match, in the dressing sheds with his arms around the little red-headed three-quarter.

> **I just loved the affection with which he spoke of his players.**

He'd been buying Brett's mum flowers and chocolates. At the Broncos, we had never thought of buying flowers and chocolates, even for Mrs Walters.

Bullfrog would pick the dominant factor in any relationship and hone in. We certainly learned from his methods, much to the delight of the Red Hill florist.

As he said to me this week, the greatest thing about his 25 years at Canterbury was that he loved every minute.

Perhaps, at times, he had his falling outs with coaches by putting his nose where it wasn't wanted, but that was simply the nature of the beast.

I just loved the affection with which he spoke of his players, particularly Terry Lamb.

There are many reasons, no doubt, for his feelings towards Lamb, but it certainly goes much deeper than a manager–player relationship, and I think that's just wonderful.

From the outside I have no doubt his two most hurtful times came with the departures of Gillespie, Langmack and Andrew Farrar and again this year, with Super League and the four players who went back to the ARL.

"Matey," he would say. "Matey, we'll sort it out."

You should see Peter Jackson impersonate him.

"Matey," says Jacko. "Matey . . ."

Canterbury were deserving winners against us last week, so very committed, and as their coach Chris Anderson rightly said, everything after St George is a bonus.

To beat the Broncos was a bonus, but to beat Canberra today? Canberra, the machine, it just goes click and hits the relentless button.

Tomorrow it's Manly and Newcastle, one rested and ready and the other wounded but rich on courage.

Manly, like the Broncos, can have an off day and that is where Newcastle's chances lie.

Only one week to go, so close to party time, and I can picture Peter Moore now, down the pointy end dishing up mineral water and health foods, teaching his players to be winners just like himself.

○ ○ ○

20.p.m.   Star ferry to Kowloon,
          Dinner @ Spring Deer, Kowloon

21. a.m.   ½ day tour

aft   Walk central/western districts

p.m   Harbour Tour.
          Drinks - Cambridge
          Dinner - Red Pepper

22 a.m   Victoria Peak.
          And Boon Haw Gdns

p.m

184